For Rowan—
With all the love in the world.

THE FRESHMAN WHO HATED SOCRATES

Dad
Nov. 07

AMHERST COLLEGE PRESS   Amherst, MA

THE FRESHMAN WHO HATED SOCRATES
A College President Reflects on Life in the Liberal Arts

Tom Gerety

Copyright © 2007 by The Trustees of Amherst College
All rights reserved.
Printed in the United States of America

ISBN 0-943184-10-X

Design by Sally Nichols
Typeset in Monotype Dante
Printed and bound by Cushing-Malloy, Inc.

For Adelia

CONTENTS

INTRODUCTION: TEACHING AS CONVERSATION … 1

BEFORE COLLEGE
Hurdles … 11
Loneliness and Learning … 17
To Paris and Back … 23
Going to America … 31

GOING TO COLLEGE
Readiness … 39
Beginnings … 45
Ambition … 51
Serious Play … 59

THE COLLEGE COMMUNITY
Roommates … 69
Of Hatred and Bridges … 81

Pilgrims, Scholars, and Hitchhikers — 89
Of Sex and Self — 97

STUDIES
In Praise of Rigor — 105
The Short Course — 111
Students and Scholars — 121
The Freshman Who Hated Socrates — 131
Lear's Wisdom — 143
Moral Teachers — 153
Heraclitus on Campus — 163
Stealing Painted Bicycles — 171

CITIZENSHIP
Country and City — 181
Mental Fight — 187
Addictions and Hypocrisies — 191
Socrates Citizen — 199
Just War — 209
Patriotisms — 215

TIME AND LOSS
Birch Beer — 225
Time's Fog — 231
Generations — 235
Time and Loss — 243

THE FRESHMAN WHO HATED SOCRATES

TEACHING AS CONVERSATION

Let me begin with praise of teaching.

The best teacher I ever had was at a small boarding school called Canterbury. His name was Roderick Clarke. I remember him then, in his mid-thirties, as a little smaller than most of us, who, at fifteen or sixteen, were awkward in our stretched-out limbs. He was a portly man, yet muscular in his shoulders and chest. His hair was short, like a monk's, but without the tonsure at the back. He went everywhere on noisy crutches with braces on his legs and shoes that laced up over the ankles. He smiled so much that the sudden seriousness of many of his comments caught me, and others, by surprise. Much of the time his face shone with the look of someone anticipating the last line of a good joke.

At supper, he would tell us, suddenly and without irony, that some remark we had made could be illuminated by a point of scholastic debate from the thirteenth century. He would say that we reminded him—in our adolescent fumbling—of the best of Ockham or perhaps the worst of Aquinas. Out of nowhere would come the counsel to go get Marc Bloch's volumes on medieval France out of our school's small library.

A lush print of Holbein's painting of Thomas More as Lord Chancellor looked down intently on our doings as we pulled out books whose authors and methods were new and alien to us. Scholarship was a strange thing to a high school sophomore. I had no sense of the days and the lives out of which such thick books would emerge. I remember still the sense of wonder at the roomy elegance of many of the footnotes in these books, these extra books to which Mr. Clarke sent me. They were like the basement apartments in New York: afterthoughts, hidden away where you barely noticed them, below the sidewalks, full of depths, of closets and cellars, each pointing the way to more unnoticed life, cellar beneath cellar in an endless deepening. This to me was the strange world of scholarship, of study crystallized into footnotes and tomes.

I have had many good teachers, more than I remember, I am sure. Mr. Clarke is the most vivid to me still.

I say all this because the best teaching I have ever known was from someone whose love for ideas—for exploration—made him not just a teacher but a scholar. And his invitation to me was an invitation not just to study, do well, and be done with it but an invitation to go on studying, endlessly and playfully, in the way of the scholar.

There is a Creole saying in Haiti: *Dèyè mon, gen mòn*. Behind the mountains, there are more mountains. For Haitians the proverb speaks of politics, where powers lurk behind powers; but I would apply it to learning. The scholar knows that learning never ends: behind its mountains there will always be more mountains.

We gather to celebrate a great tradition of learning. The beginning we make today marks, in a small way, the continuing, here and elsewhere, of that tradition. The college, small as it is now, frail as it was for most of its first several decades—the college stands for the very best within our tradition of study and teaching. If I may speak not for myself but for Amherst, then Amherst, in turn, must speak not only for itself, but for the liberal arts tradition.

Teaching is where we must begin: in the peculiarly human relation of the teacher and the student, the one who knows and the one who would know, the one who has the discipline that comes of long, concentrated study and the one who seeks it. Often, as we all know, it is the student who teaches the teacher. Ideas are the most volatile of cultural substances, and they move among minds with an almost magical quality of speed and surprise. Our task is to structure that magic, to give it rigor and discipline.

It was in August of 1821 that Amherst's first president, Zephaniah Moore, rode down from Williamstown to found this college. His horse had its tail and mane cropped by the angry students and townspeople he left behind. Since then, he and his successors have stated and restated what this college meant to them. For more than a hundred years the meaning was chiefly religious. Put here for the education of indigent young men of piety and talents for the Christian ministry, Amherst was in effect a missionary college. Its purpose, in the words of our motto, *Terras irradient,* was to illuminate the many lands of the globe with an understanding of the one true faith.

We are a long, long way from such certainty about our mission. There was a self-evidence, a sometimes uncritical self-certainty, in who and what we were one hundred and fifty years ago. The religious creed itself, in which our faculty and students labored, was debated, of course. Indeed, the religious controversy made a decisive contribution: Amherst was founded in the dual conviction that Harvard was God-forsaken in its doctrines—and Williams in its location.

We must take care to avoid any arrogance, or even complacency, in our own convictions, our own faiths. Yet we should emulate the passion of our founders, and recognize that we too must ground our work in some faith.

Let me take our story back farther than Amherst itself.

In the beginning, wrote John Locke in the *Second Treatise of Government,* all the world was America. Locke meant to capture in this sentence the wildness of nature, including human nature, in the condition that preceded civil

INTRODUCTION

society. But he caught as well a sense of Europe and America as strangers: encountering one another on the edge of this continent, on the shorelines to the east of us and in the woods that surround us still. This America, the America of strangeness and difference, was to produce many innovations, some wonderful and some horrible: slavery; the decimation and subjugation of the native peoples we encountered here; the sweatshops of our cities and the bigotry of our laws. All these were horrors. But they do not blot out the wonders: our music with its looseness and force; our poetry with its openness and oddity; our humor, our enterprise, our astounding if only occasional generosity as a people.

One of America's most lasting innovations was a written constitution. We were the first to interpret the written words of a fundamental law as binding on even the most powerful among us. Constitutional law, open to debate and to change, but upheld by judges backed by the might of the government—this was new and even now remains wonderful. Among our inventions, no less new or wondrous, no less American in Locke's sense, I would place the liberal arts college.

We know that universities grew up in Europe long before Europeans settled here. And we know that the colleges—the special residence halls at Paris and Oxford, at Cambridge and Bologna—developed within the universities along with their great faculties. The liberal arts college began here as a religious school. In it, the arts of the free citizen—the liberal arts—were subsumed under the religious mission not only of the school but of the society as a whole. Amherst was not much different in this in the 1820s from Harvard in the 1630s or Yale in the 1700s.

Up until the Civil War, the liberal arts college more or less defined higher education in America. Then all the world was Amherst. Harvard and Yale, Princeton and Columbia, Williams and Trinity and Union: all were colleges of roughly similar size and ambition. Some were more secular and some more innovative than others. Some, like Oberlin and Swarthmore and Berea, put women on an equal basis with men. They, along with Amherst, challenged the rest of America to set aside race as a qualification for study.

Others, like Mount Holyoke and later Smith, Wellesley, and many others, pushed the country to honor women's abilities and ambitions.

Then began the great expansion, public and private, that was to remake the landscape in higher education. Suddenly, universities were everywhere, with a variety of faculties, graduate and professional as well as undergraduate, and all with a new sense of mission and a new confidence about their relation to the country's future. The land grant colleges made possible the emergence of large public universities like the University of Massachusetts. The founding of Johns Hopkins spurred our Ivy League brethren to grow into collections of schools, with the undergraduate colleges prominent but no longer truly dominant.

By the 1880s, a Columbia professor could write that the colleges were finished, caught between boarding schools and the new universities. It will be largely a waste of capital to maintain them, he declared, and largely a waste of time to attend them.

The universities saved us from a narrow parochial world that threatened to smother what it once had nurtured. Electives, majors, research: all these began in the transatlantic dialogue that transformed higher education. It became a massive engine that could serve the nation and the world as no liberal arts college could hope to. The sheer scale of the enterprise was beyond us. Responding to the massive shift around us, we struggled to retain a sense of purpose. It was not easy; it would never be easy again.

Where once Amherst and schools like it educated the great majority of those Americans who were to lead in government and the professions, in business and the arts, now we educate only a slight fraction of those who study beyond high school. The question of our purpose sharpens: Why should the liberal arts college—not just Amherst but the family of such colleges—why should the liberal arts college survive and prosper? In the age of the university, what have we to offer our students and the world?

The answer to my questions lies in the conjunction, the radical conjunction, of teaching and learning: we in the liberal arts colleges believe that teacher and student must stand face to face in the many conversations that

INTRODUCTION

are the work of both; we believe in teaching as conversation because the best teaching *is* conversation; only through dialogue can we do our work.

The college, unlike the university, takes the dialogue of professor and student as a master principle. Neither graduate students nor teaching assistants can spell us in this central portion of our vocation. Our scale and our intimacy, our flexibility in moving across and among fields, our openness to one another and to our students—these are the strengths of a community built on dialogue. Yes, we are specialists, but we are also generalists: intellectuals first, with a curiosity that does not stop at the boundaries of one discipline but pushes on to ask about the disciplines of our colleagues.

The temptation, from afar, is to say that scholarship in such a setting must be slighted in favor of teaching. But Amherst, with others, holds that these are complementary aspects of one vocation.

One *can* teach, perhaps, with more or less permanent authority from a fixed store of learning.

That sort of teaching holds little interest here. We teach instead what we learn and as we learn—not once and for all but over and again, renewing our knowledge *as* we test it and push it and extend it. There is an important sense in which, at their very best, teaching and research become one. The best teaching searches out new questions and new insights; and the best research always teaches.

Half a century ago, when my teacher Roderick Clarke was a freshman at Amherst, he met professors like yours. I doubt if even Mr. Clarke could remember much of what they said in those hectic days right after the Second World War. What we recall of our teachers is rarely the lore—the fact of this or that, the rule of physics, the declension of a noun, the acquaintance with a book or poem. We take away something more elusive and more important.

From Mr. Clarke I took a sense of the play of ideas, his joy in them, but also of his insistence on rigor and discipline in embracing them. He once gave me an A on a first draft of a paper on the Spanish Armada. I typed it up more or less as it was for the final submission. I was distraught to learn that the final draft—and the grade—was a B or B+. You didn't take it far, he told me. You didn't take it anywhere.

We are here because we seek a learning we can take somewhere, a learning we can take with us into our lives. It is not a gift but an acquisition, requiring discipline as well as imagination. Mr. Clarke, however joyous, however playful, was the sternest of teachers. In a difficult time, with many who doubt the uses of colleges such as this, we must be clear about our work.

We gather today around a library on a beautiful hill, in the midst of laboratories and theaters, fields and museums. Ours is an old conversation, but we must make it new for every student and in every classroom. We must make it as open as possible—to ideas, of course, but to people as well, to our differences, to our clashes of conviction, of style, of temperament and background. Ultimately, ours is a conversation about who we are and what we can do in our world. It is about freedom and what we can make of it. It is about reality and how we can understand it. It is about the imagination and how it can draw us toward wisdom—and toward one another.

To all who would study in this tradition, we say: come to Amherst if you would join us in this work. Never mind whether you are rich or poor. Never mind where or how you live. Say only that you would bring to this conversation all of your curiosity, your intelligence, your passion. Say that you would engage with others in argument and exploration wherever it leads. Say that whatever else you do with your life you would take learning to heart as your calling, the calling of the scholar, the teacher, and the student.

I am proud to join you in this work and adventure.

BEFORE COLLEGE

Hurdles

I went to school in the Connecticut woods, over hills and the Housatonic River, at the end of the roads that wend west. I remember still the round-faced yellow bus that chugged up and down the dark roads overhung with hemlock, toward contests whose outcomes I have long forgotten. Through the steep shadows and the shafts of sunlight the bus seemed always to rush. It was cold in the bus, even on a warm October Saturday. Steel pipes framed the seats, and they were cold, and so was the brown Naugahyde. We would drive up to the gym in the bright sunlight and climb from the bus blinking and silent. We were a grim and uncertain line of boys, shuffling along with bags full of pads and cleats. One boy would pretend to laugh at something that struck no one else as funny. Our coach, whose world embraced much more than ours, would talk quietly and without anxiety. But even *his* voice seemed chaste and tentative. We would go on into the dressing rooms, undress slowly, suit up and make our way onto the broad, bright field.

There was a school with a reputation for a nearly Spartan toughness. They did not win every game, but they won more than enough. I hurdled in those days. They had a hurdler, a post graduate I think, who must have stood six inches higher than I. We talked before the race in the laconic tones of boys wary of each other's prowess. He ran seven strides between hurdles, I ran nine; my legs were simply not long enough. I thought of myself as a pretty good hurdler, but I knew this lean muscular young man was an entirely different sort of athlete.

My coach was my Latin teacher, Mr. Breen; he was later to become a headmaster. All I remember from him that day was a smile that said "try." It also said, "I know, the odds are overwhelming." I beat that hurdler to the first set of hurdles; the start was always my best shot. But at each row after that I lost a yard or so. That tall hurdler finished ten yards in front, a full second ahead of me. I went back to Canterbury humbled, but determined to do better. Evenings after supper I'd go up to the track and try for seven steps. It was an awkward, silly gait for me, at five foot ten inches. Seven steps of mine just wouldn't cover ten yards, not at full speed, not with any kind of grace over the hurdles. So I tried eight. It meant I had to change my leg at each row of hurdles. I worked on that alternating stride all spring.

To end the season, we had a meet to which several schools came, including his. Four of us lined up for the first heat. The tall hurdler was there, next to me in the lane. Again I went over the first hurdle first. This time I had my eight strides to give me hope. He too had worked hard that spring. He strode next to me with an almost scythe like force. He took each hurdle the way I imagine you would cut wheat: cleanly, flatly, quietly—almost imperceptibly. At each hurdle he gained a foot or two. The two others in the heat, in the far lanes, ran a fast backdrop to my race with this hurdler. They beat me, but I scarcely noticed. Perhaps he's still running and hurdling now; if so, I salute him. I salute him because he taught me something. He taught about *trying*, about trying my best whatever the odds. A great teacher I once knew named this the Effort System, and institutionalized it with his students. "You fail at Trinity Pawling," the *Student Handbook* there says, "only when you fail to try."

When the race was over we had a new league record—more than a full second better than our own school record. I finished fourth in that four-man heat. Each of the three hurdlers ahead of me clocked in at least a half-second better than the school record. At ten yards back from the great hurdler I knew that I had run my fastest race ever. I went up to Mr. Shea, my history teacher, the timekeeper, to ask what my time was. I secretly hoped to have broken a school record. He told me they had clocked the first three runners. I ran a lot of races as a kid: the 220, the 440, relays, the hurdles. I pole-vaulted. I won some of those races. The race I remember best is this one: in a heat in which I came in last, in which no clock recorded my time, I ran the best hurdles race of my life. Mr. Breen knew this, I suspect; Mr. Shea *may* have known it. What mattered most was that *I* knew it. All those evenings alone on the track; the risk I took in switching from nine steps on one leg to eight on both; the sheer yearning of all those hours of practice. All of it came to this: victory in an inward race, victory not over anyone else, but only over the hurdles themselves, and victory somehow over *myself*. By *trying* to win, I had won.

The ideal of a school, the ideal your teachers are called to champion, is this: only in discipline and perseverance will you have—*can* you have—such victories, true and lasting victories, victories that are yours because they are victories in the great human struggle for meaning.

It is an important and different question why that should be. We measure lots of things in life by measures outside ourselves: births, deaths; degrees, jobs; grades; wealth; these are all measures outside ourselves. None of these measures will give meaning to your life. Human beings are so constructed—I'm not sure why—that above all other things, beyond wealth or power or glory, or even love itself, we crave *meaning:* a sense of purpose, and a satisfaction in that purpose that no one can take away. At its limit, that craving for meaning is religious, a craving for purposes given by God.

A psychologist who studied Nobel Prize winners found that virtually all of them ran into a wall of despair *after* they won, in the wake of their achievement. "What's left?" they wondered. "What mountain is there to be scaled?"

Purposes differ from achievements; purposes must outlast the achievements they inspire; and purposes, especially large and generous purposes, give a satisfaction beyond any achievement.

Students must find out all of this the hard way, in their own lives. Their parents and teachers will try to tell them, but they may not listen. They may have felt it already at the end of a good game or a good season, at the end of a summer or a job well done. When it's over, whatever you have achieved, you have to pick up and move on. Winning and losing are not that far apart; neither permits us to linger.

The worst thing about all this is how lonely it can be. Even the most popular kid you know can't really take his purposes from his crowd. Friends *can* help, but they're searching too. Teamwork isn't so lonely. You *can* struggle with your teammates to achieve a common purpose—a goal or a touchdown, a winning season. But a team's common purpose ends with its season. You realize when it's over that it meant something to you only if you can make the qualities of the team your *personal* qualities, drawing into yourself what it was that made the team good: pulling together, trying like crazy, hanging in there right to the end. You have to do this not just on the playing field, with a coach, an umpire, a crowd, but off the field, too; because most of life is off the field. Its meaning won't show up on any scoreboard I know.

"Life," said Justice Holmes, "is painting a picture." What he did not say is that the picture you paint is of yourself.

These years of school, years in which your bodies grow from childhood to adulthood, years in which the mind alternates between elation and despair, these years are like the sketches for an adult picture of one's self. All the effort students make—studying subjects they do not like, working at chores, trying to get along with a difficult classmate or teacher—all that effort will sometimes seem wasted. "I'm just doing this to get through," you say to yourself in gloomier moments. What we may not realize is how much these efforts strengthen the lines and details of our self-portraits.

The self you will become must be a joyful self, one that takes joy from the things you love—sports or music, books, or invention. It must also be a self that sticks to it, that won't back down or give up. Courage, said Churchill, is the virtue on which all the rest depend. You won't be there for your friends unless you have courage. And courage begins with standing by your own sense of what's right.

The rigor and discipline of a school is above all an attitude of mind, a posture of intellect and will. Education is directed to the formation of character. A foot race is a test of character too. But in the long stretch of life that takes you from the time when you were a baby to your own age now, on to college and adulthood—in that long stretch, races and games, interviews and admissions, successes and rejections, all will run together and disappear, like the scores of the games I played. All this will blur as stray moments, bits of color in the painting that is your character. That character will need the frame and outline imposed on it in a school.

When you leave here you will go to college. Whatever choice you make, college will be hard, but more than hard, college will be free. You will be on your own, choosing not just your courses and your friends, but your whole way of living. Professors will notice if you don't come to class. But for the most part you will be on your own.

"Did you get a good roommate?" I asked a freshman this fall. "I got a single," she told me. Her answer made my question all the more pointed. Whoever else joins you in your room, you room for life with yourself. Your character is with you in all that you do. Make sure it is the character you want: strong, sensible, and generous, thoughtful about values, attentive to others and decent to one and all. Character is man's fate, wrote the ancient Greek Heraclitus. Make *your* fate a good one.

Loneliness and Learning

The boarding school I went to had a stone chapel set high on a hill. Chapel was required in those days, every night before supper. It seemed to me then that it was always dark as we made our way up what I remember now as hundreds of steps. We wore gray flannel suits in the evenings; they itched. Our shirts and ties felt too tight around our collars. Sometimes, though, the sky was glorious in its darkening, streaked in fall and even winter with the colors of spring blossoms, purples and oranges and reds and a silver brightness in the clouds.

I was lonely from the first. Oh, there were a few heady hours: keep-away and Frisbees and boys to play with and talk to (I had grown up in the solitude of the country). But soon I felt alone, grimly alone. I missed the milk in the refrigerator, the pretzels in the pantry, the chance to watch television or go to bed when I felt like it. I was homesick—deeply, agonizingly homesick.

I knew that I was supposed to be more grown up; boarding was my own idea, after all. But the loneliness dug so deep into me that I felt the only cure for it was to leave. The thought came to me that if I remained homesick—chronically, incurably homesick—I would be able to make the case to my parents that I had to quit and I had to go home. So I began to pray in the chapel that God would keep me homesick at least until my parents came to visit.

Each night in the chapel I would linger on my knees until all but the most pious had gone down to supper. "Please, God," I would say, "keep me homesick, hard as it is, so that I can show my parents that they have to take me home."

Parents Weekend must have been at an eternal remove—two weeks or more, I would guess—from the impatient fourteen-year-old that I was then. Each night I feared that the next morning I would wake up to find my homesickness gone and my imagined escape foreclosed.

In the paradoxical logic that was mine, to get over my homesickness would be the worst fate I could encounter. When that happened (and I knew deep down that it would happen soon) I would be forced to make a go of it.

Finally, Parents Weekend came, and I plotted how to tell my parents of my loneliness and of my desperation to go home. Somewhere near school there was a white clapboard inn. I remember still the shiny cars in the parking lot and the glasses of ice water on the tablecloths. "I have to go home," I said to my mother and father. "Why?" they asked. I went through my reasons, all props and symbols of my loneliness. I concluded with my homesickness.

My mother asked gently if there wasn't some way to make it work. "We could visit more often." "Can't you buy cookies?" My father listened for a time. Her face was worried and mobile; his seemed to me still and pensive. We had talked for a time and were ordering from the menu. When the waiter left, my father looked at me and said: "You chose it and you'll stick it out until the end of the year."

I am sure that I never felt so alone. My parents would no longer rescue me from my own choices. It was the beginning for me of adulthood. By the next morning, as if there had been some miracle, my homesickness was gone. No more excuses kept it alive. I was on my own.

I want to say a few words to you about loneliness and going your own way. You can't have one without the other.

As you leave this place today you will feel that you leave behind a bit of yourself. The years you have been here, the friends you have had here, your teachers, these buildings, the trees and fields—all of this you will put behind you because you have finished your work here. Now you must move on to other places and other people. It will feel lonely; you, too, will be homesick, if only a little, for this school and those you have known here.

Before, for the most part, you were on your way home whenever you left. That may be true even today. But your parents know—and you must feel—that the ground is shifting in your lives.

"Going home" is less and less the true description of your destination. Because what you are doing, today and in the days to come, is really setting out. And what you're heading toward is adulthood, your own adult self, shaped and toughened to last through a lifetime of changes.

You won't remember much of what I say today, so I'll make it simple. You'll always miss what you leave behind. Sometimes you'll miss it so much that you won't want to push on. But you have to. You can't stay put—not here, nor in a sense anywhere. And as you push on you will be lonely, sometimes as lonely as the September third-former who stands shyly at the edge of the senior green or watches in the parking lot by the rink as last year's varsity team comes back from summer. I want you to understand that loneliness is the companion of learning, of growing and growing up.

You cannot set out to learn something new and difficult unless you are willing to be on your own, cut off a bit from your friends and parents and even your teachers. The harder the lesson you seek to learn, the lonelier you will feel as you work to master it. New lessons, new worlds, rarely open themselves to any who are not explorers and adventurers, willing to leave what is familiar, to light out, as Huck Finn said, for the territory, by which he meant the frontier, the unexplored, unconquered territory: the wilderness.

There are all kinds of wildernesses, within as well as without. Don't be scared by any of them.

I once stole a nickel from a glass jar that my grandmother kept on a sideboard. I felt guilty about it late that night, long after I had spent it on gum and candy. I believed in hell then and thought that if I were to die that night, with that sin unconfessed on my soul, I would go straight to hell and stay there forever. That night I broke out into a sweat. Who knows if I had a summer flu? I got up in the dark and my mother called out to me. "I have a fever, Mom, I think I need an aspirin." She told me to take a glass of water instead.

The next morning the sun came up bright and clear; a breeze from the water stirred the leaves. My night of fever seemed by daylight a nightmare; I was glad to be done with it. Later that morning I told Grandma that I had taken the nickel and spent it; she said I had made good use of it. Hell seemed a long way off. By daylight I saw what I had done with another's eyes, Grandma's. If there was a hell somewhere out there for the wicked caught up by death in their wickedness it was probably too important a place for the likes of me. I learned something that night, and it wasn't simply to leave Grandma's nickels where I found them. A week or two later I found myself arguing with my uncle, the priest, about the soul and its fate after death. I was no longer sure that a just god would send a little boy to hell for stealing nickels or lying to his mother. I wasn't even sure there was a soul left after death. "Maybe we go *poof* and vanish," I remember saying to my uncle Jack, who sat there with his round collar on. Grandma came in on my side when an aunt tried to shush my questioning of church doctrine. My uncle gave me pretty good answers; but I held my ground, certain not so much of where I stood as of the questions I wanted to ask before I took up a position of my own.

I had spent a night in close proximity to damnation and survived with a strong sense that my convictions ought to be my own.

Loneliness is the price of individuality. We *are* alone, each of us, in our thoughts and bodies and selves. And yet at the same time we are necessarily part of families and schools and communities. The paradox in this is that we must learn to move back and forth between the self on its own, independent and choosing, and the self together with others, needing them (and being needed by them) and keeping them in mind.

This is the essential rhythm of human life and thought: a shuttling back and forth between the self you are and the selves that others are. It is with those other selves that you must work and play, build families and homes, nations—and a world.

I say all this to you now because of where you are in your own lives. You've come a long way, I know. Most of you are as big as you'll ever be, as full of energy and strength and intelligence. In many things you know exactly what you want.

But I suspect that many of you wonder, a little nervously, what's up ahead.

College is a kind of a bridge to adulthood. Not an ordinary bridge, though, of stone and concrete, wood and steel. It's more of a rope bridge, strong enough in its way to get you across the river, but a bridge that requires effort and imagination to get across, that forces you to keep your own sense of balance as you move ahead. You'll be tempted to get across in a hurry, with a great leap of one kind or another. You'll look across to the other side—a long way, really—and say to yourself something that in retrospect will seem foolish or worse. "Adults can handle their liquor in great quantities," some of you will say to yourselves, usually in your first semester of college. You'll be acting like a freshman, stupidly and naively, but you'll be telling yourself that this is being grown up, and free, and having fun.

Some of you will reason in this way about sexuality. "Adults can handle sex more or less like liquor," you'll think. "They indulge when they want to, with whom they please, and then they move on."

And so it goes. There is a wonderful Latin word for all of this: simulacrum. These are the simulacra—the tricked-up, phony, fake versions of what you want. You want to be on your own; you want to be free and smart; and you want to take responsibility for your own life in a way that you have never done before.

All of this will happen in the next few months and years, for all of you.

The boundary is clear. Yes, high school and your families may have given you an increasing measure of freedom over the last few years. Most of you learned to drive and do research papers and hold a summer job. But all of this is a preparation. The real freedom begins with college. For in almost every college in the land there will be enough freedom to make an absolute disaster of any moment in the next several years of your life.

Date rape, racial insults, alcohol poisonings, and petty vandalisms and destructions. Invite the college security chief to speak to you—instead of the president—and ask him what sorts of adventures fill up his days and nights.

Out of this freedom you *can*—most of you *will*—make something lasting and wonderful. You'll find a subject of study that will draw you on toward a life's work or a great ideal; you'll find a friend who will last for years, or a romance that becomes the love of your life; you'll learn that you're good at numbers or ideas or politics. You'll travel in imagination and reality to places far away and difficult, places that you will come to know only with the lonely effort of speaking another language and understanding another culture.

These possibilities make up the complex architecture of the bridge that I mentioned before. In a great poem about a bridge, Hart Crane wrote of "the choiring strings" that suspend the Brooklyn Bridge over the East River. Whenever I read that line I think not of the actual cables of a bridge but of ropes hung from branches over a river near my home. You swing out over the water and then let go. It's a lonely but joyous moment as you fly down into the water before you splash and swim.

Maybe that's the better image for you and for your crossing over the river to adulthood. There will be moments of great joy, but often lonely moments, and then the splash of choice, and then the hard swim across in the currents. Remember that you are on your own, that your choices matter, and that your joys will never be true unless you have earned them with a measure of loneliness.

To Paris and Back

I did not come by a high school diploma entirely honestly. Here is how it happened.

The summer after my junior year I went on a coal boat—*un bateau à charbon,* the captain called it—to France. My brother Peter came along. For nine days we ploughed the green Atlantic, endless fog, and the eccentric idioms of a captain who compared every dish served to a woman he had known. We landed at last in Le Havre, staying only long enough to catch the last train. Not much after dawn the overnight train brought Paris into view, with Sacré Coeur and Montmartre high up, catching the light and spilling it down on the rest of the city below. Peter and I stood at the train window—the ones that say don't fall out, *ne pas se pencher*—and our hearts fell out and ran ahead on the tracks to whatever it was Paris held for us. It was Hemingway who wrote of the luck, the moveable feast, of living in Paris as a young man. I felt very lucky.

That summer was mostly language lessons, at the Institut Catholique. I had my own room with a balcony looking across the Seine to Notre Dame. I read out loud for hours, armed with determination and a dictionary. I imagined that I wasn't a sixteen-year-old kid in summer school, but a poet, a wanderer, a philosopher. I studied harder than I ever had. My French teachers at Canterbury, a Catholic boarding school in Connecticut, had taught me plenty. All I needed to complete my fantasy was to jump from school French to fluency—and in a couple of months I did.

In August, I wrote home to ask if I could stay the year. To my father this meant an unwelcome end to touchdowns and track meets. It was only when he showed my letters to another Canterbury parent, a lawyer named Richard Joyce Smith, that I won a sympathetic hearing. Mr. Smith convinced my father that this was too good a chance to pass up. Yes, I could stay. So I enrolled in the philosophy class in the only lycée that would have me, Jeanson-de-Sailly, in the Sixteenth Arrondissement.

Toward the end of the year Mr. Sheehan, the headmaster, wrote to say I should come back to Canterbury to graduate. I was surprised, and embarrassed. My schoolwork at the lycée was haphazard: full of intellectual tangents, odd passions, and loneliness. I read Simone Weil, Descartes and Pascal, Nietzsche and Sartre. I read novel after novel but barely looked at the yellowed science text and did nothing in math beyond memorizing a few formulas. In the required English class my American accent made me useless to the teacher.

When I came back to Canterbury, I spent one night in a dorm, fending off questions from envious classmates. The next day, as the seniors gathered in line, the tackle on the football team said loudly, to no one in particular, "Gerety spends the whole year playing around in Paris while I stay here killing myself to make it through physics and history. Then he waltzes in to pick up a diploma. It's just not fair."

It was *not* fair. But I smiled secretly then, and I smile openly now; my classmate must long ago have forgiven Canterbury—and me—the injustice. As in the parable of the workers in the vineyard, we took away the same wages for unequal labors.

You could write the history of Canterbury as the history of an American school that happened to be Catholic; I could write my own history that way too. In both cases, though, mine and Canterbury's, the history would lack something vital, even causal. Catholicism shaped us both. It is in our bones, our intellectual bones, if not always rising to consciousness.

For most of us, as for Canterbury, our story is in part about an evolving relationship between the religion, the faith, of our family and the world we encountered in growing up—an American world full of ideas, conflicts, uncertainties. Or to put this more simply, it is a story about the relation between a given faith and the self, the ornery, free-standing, opinionated self.

My relation to Canterbury seems to me now something like Canterbury's relation to Catholicism. I was attached to it, even passionately attached to it; but I was also restless within it, jealously guarding my own prerogatives of reflection and judgment. Above all, I wanted to be independent. I was eager to judge for myself and to experience for myself what was out there in the world.

I had had to argue my way into Canterbury, just as I was later to argue my way out. One of my brothers, after a lackadaisical year in fourth form, had not been asked back. No one in my family thought I needed to board. Since it was my idea, at thirteen, it was a primitive idea: I would go to Canterbury not to redeem the family record but because I wanted to go to boarding school. And Canterbury was the one school I wanted. My father's answer was plain: I didn't need to go away and he wasn't prepared to send me—unless I won a scholarship. And so I came—through a maze of leafy roads and clapboard villages, up from the coast where we lived to inland New Milford, past Lincoln's bust at the bottom of the hill, up Aspetuck Avenue to the crest, and down the drive to North House. The first night, there was a mist in the forest to the west; an army of boys played keep-away with a coonskin cap; it was heaven, with only a hint of homesickness.

When two laymen founded Canterbury, in 1915, their vision was an upstart one, in at least two senses. First, it was upstart because they set themselves up in the face of a lingering prejudice against Catholics in the universities and boarding schools that set the standard for higher education in America.

Second, and perhaps more interesting, it was an upstart vision within the Church. This was to be a Catholic school, yet a Catholic school run by laymen and not much beholden, in its founding or direction, to the hierarchy or to the great religious orders. It was a school within a tradition, and yet not quite like anything else in that tradition.

From John Carroll to John Kennedy and on to Mario Cuomo and many others, there has been a tension in American Catholicism between the authority of the Church—hierarchical, absolutist, and European—and the legitimacy of our democracy—egalitarian, individualistic, and, above all, American. It is a healthy tension. Still it gives rise to misunderstandings. It leads to real perplexity whenever the Church asserts its teaching authority in public life. The abortion controversy is a case in point. The Church has a view, an absolute view. Many disagree with that view, and want no part of it in politics. Yet the Church cannot be the Church unless from time to time it asserts its views. "But it costs nothing to have an opinion," says an aged character in the Australian novel *Just Relations*, "and if you've got no opinions where's your civilization?" The Church must have its opinions, its positions; and the Church must teach them. When it does, the question arises: how should we, as citizens of this democracy *and* members of the Church, receive these teachings? Some would say that we should receive them without a murmur of deliberation or a moment of hesitation. Yet conscience does not work that way. Active, intelligent conscience requires independence of mind.

Canterbury's founding was an answer to the question: how can we be good Americans and good Catholics at the same time? In a good school—as in a good country—thought runs free, on its own course, to its own conclusions. Canterbury was founded to be Catholic *and* to be free, to balance the authority of the Church with the reflections of independent minds.

During that spring in Paris, I heard about the great student pilgrimage to the cathedral of Chartres. I went along not out of piety but out of romance. Thousands of students from all over Europe gathered outside Paris to walk and sing and talk their way to Chartres. We camped somewhere in the fields, around small fires. We talked the way many French do, with madcap fluency, in concepts precisely stated yet vast and uncertain. The topic around our campfire was the difficulty of living like the saints of old. A measure of fatalism in the discussion troubled me. A bright Belgian student said that the modern world made it impossible to be a saint. "We can't be like St. Francis or St. Clare," she said, "not in the world as we know it." Younger than she, and full of doubts about my own faith, I hesitated to say what I thought. Yet I chafed at her resigned and complacent tone. I thought Christianity should be passionate and headlong. I protested suddenly as I might have in Father Ryan's theology class at Canterbury. I remember the word risk—*risque*—and the claim that nothing important had changed since the time of Francis and Clare. It was a stirring debate. A lean, soft-spoken African student came to my defense. We argued on into the night. The fire burned down and its light made a gold rim on the hay behind us. The next evening as we marched on to Chartres, you could see far ahead the bands of students turning and turning on the narrow streets, up the hill to the great cathedral. Never had I believed in Christianity more than then, when argument drew me to its defense, and more argument drew me on toward belief.

Augustine speaks, rightly, of faith seeking reason. There is also reason—or if that's too French a word, *experience*—seeking faith.

Surely if the Catholic Church errs, it errs in the direction of a central and hierarchic authority. Aquinas warned that the argument from authority is always the weakest. You may say that Canterbury, never challenged authority, or much protested against it. Yet I went to a school where faith was never blind.

It was a school that gave us all an acquaintance with absolutes. As a religious school, how could it not? The religions that interest me, said a rabbi, should tell us what to do with our pots and pans and our sexuality. Perhaps all religions should acquaint us with absolutes. Catholics, whatever the state of our beliefs, are at home with absolutes; we say, and the Church says, that we should live by them. We have grown up thinking that way.

Yet there is something in our tradition that keeps us from too easy an embrace of absolutism. I am not sure what it is that holds us back: irony perhaps, or a sense of time and the way it makes all lives fragile. For me, it was above all my teachers who tempered the absolutism of adolescence with wonder and wisdom. In Canterbury's teaching there was a ferocity and a passion suggesting absolute horizons. But there was then, and I know there remains, a skepticism, a questioning, and a willingness to yield fixed positions. We were taught to search and search hard before settling upon answers. This school was for me, and for many others, a crucible of identity. Canterbury's teachers knew that, and taught what they taught with patience and humor as well as zeal.

"More years ago than I like now to remember," wrote Judge Learned Hand on his return to Harvard Law School, "I sat in this building and listened to—yes, more than that, was dissected by—men all but one of whom are now dead." Most of *my* Canterbury teachers live on still: many still teach. They have grown a little grayer, but no gentler, no less dissecting. They were probers and dissectors all of them, hard teachers, knotty and deep-grained, like splinters of wood, with a resin and strength and sharpness all their own.

What Hand took from his teachers, he said, was not so much the rules or facts they lectured on. What I took from mine was not an explanation of the defenestration at Prague or Caesar's narrative methods, not an account of the navigation of bats or of the Byronic hero in each of us. "I carried away," said Hand, "the impress of a band of devoted scholars . . . whom nothing could daunt and nothing could bribe. . . . In the universe of truth they lived by the sword; they asked no quarter of absolutes and they gave none." Never before or since have I known such teachers: fierce, unyielding masters of words and numbers, ideas and ideals.

Even their mercies stunned me. I will never forget the A one gave me for writing my test left-handed after I broke my right arm. More than once, my Latin teacher disregarded the grammatical liberties of my translations of Caesar to praise their style and sense; for that I thank him. One evening at dinner one asked what I thought of the film *How Green Was My Valley*. "Uncomfortable," I told him, because I had squirmed in my seat throughout.

I will never forget his praise of that one word. It opened up a world to me.

We are all teachers, in our way. Human culture is a vast classroom, or better a great school full of classrooms of every description. Our species may be defined in many ways—by its words, by its lengthy childhood, by its aspirations of faith and reason. Forgive me if I, as a teacher, say that we are first and last a teaching species. To be human is to teach: the parent, the priest; the carpenter and gardener; the businesswoman; Sojourner Truth and Abraham Lincoln; Roderick Clarke and lots of others. All of us, in our best moments, teach one another.

I will leave you with the recollection of an hour at Canterbury in the early springtime of 1963. It was Mr. Clarke's history class. In all his classes, Mr. Clarke assigned roles, so we became the players on history's stage. He would allot these roles, these fates, with what seemed a casual indifference: "You're the peasant Bodo; you're Madame Eglantine," and then, to a particularly unadventurous fifth-former, *"You* are the great Venetian explorer, Marco Polo." We laughed, we hooted, we were delighted.

Medieval history is steeped as dark as Irish tea in the Church and its mysteries; the cast of characters is endless; and Clarke loved to set us thinking with his choices for us. One day he populated an entire kingdom with members of our class. One was king and one was lord; one a banker; one a bishop; one a soldier and one a peasant. Each assignment brought laughter, then questions, and lengthy commentaries on the prospects of this new denizen of the French Middle Ages.

Conn Nugent and I were intellectual rivals and friends. We sat at the back murmuring objections as all life's great parts were dispensed and digested. Only toward the end of class did Mr. Clarke peer back at the two of us. We still awaited our assignments. "And you, Conn Nugent; and you, Tom Gerety: what of you?" He paused with a great flourish of suspense and delight. Then, intoning each word, he said: "You two will be friars of the Cistercian Abbey of *Je-ne-sais-où.*" He had hardly let out the words before Nugent jumped up in exuberant protest. "Absurd! Never! Not on my life!" And then I asked: "Why us?" "Because," Mr. Clarke said, "you are such good students that you have no need of titles or fortunes or even a plot of land; you will make your way with only your minds."

I recall the bell ringing dully, books and desks slamming, the feet of classmates shuffling out toward the next class, the next adventure.

Conn and I smiled at each another and exulted.

Going to America

I had a great-uncle in Ireland. He lived in the little village of Creggs in County Galway, where he kept a store. When my wife and I visited him years ago, he was ninety or so. He sat atop a tall stool with a cane in hand, and bragged of his own youthfulness next to villagers ten or twenty years younger. "I can still dance and laugh while they are stiff and sad," he told us.

He recalled a party, perhaps eighty years before, for his brother, my grandfather. "We stayed up all night," he said. "We danced and talked and laughed, and in the morning we said our good-byes." He called it a Going-to-America party. His thirteen-year-old brother was off to the seaport and the sea—bound for America.

When you finish high school you have a graduation ceremony—several days of laughter and dance and talk and tears. This for you is a type of Going-to-America party. Only the America you're headed toward is adulthood, the dread state your parents seem so hopelessly mired in when you want to borrow the car or stay out all night. I don't have much to say about adulthood. It's all right, as far as it goes. You'll find out all about it when you arrive.

I want to talk about the passage over, the sea between *you* now and *you* later, and my sense of what you will feel and see and do (or not see and do) in the great crossing before you, the long, stormy passage after childhood and yet before adulthood.

What lies before you is a kind of freedom-time. Most of you will leave home for college. Don't take much with you; it'll weigh you down.

These will be the freest years you ever live.

Neither your parents nor your teachers will hover over you as they have until now. If you've chosen a college like the one I went to, you'll be free to stay up all night, to eat all day or not at all, to work in fits and starts. You'll be free not because no one will depend on you. Many of us—friends, teachers, teammates, families—many of us will still depend on you. You'll be free because you can *choose*—readily, freely, crazily—whom you'd like to study with, talk with, hang out with, whom you think you should depend on and who should depend on you. When you're done with college, there will be professions, careers, families of your own awaiting you. This freedom-time keeps you clear of all that. These several years before you will unfold as an endless succession of possibilities. You could try them *all* out. But what I want to tell you is that as you do, you will choose who you are. "If all of life is an experiment," as Justice Holmes once said, then surely all of college is an experiment in selfhood, a passage to adulthood.

Nowhere else in the world do we arrange things in quite this way. In all of Europe and Asia and Africa and Latin America students at colleges and universities study in one field, almost always a field of lifelong professional choice. In America we dabble. We *postpone* professional choice. We experiment with possible lives. We make the passage from childhood to adulthood a lengthy and complicated one, a free one, and in some ways a dangerous one.

Surely each of you has been surprised, sometime in the last several years, to find yourself suddenly looking *down*—or at least eye-to-eye—at a teacher, a parent, a friend: someone who used to look down from great heights at you. Your feet, your limbs, your *selves* have all suddenly, stunningly, grown up. The shoes don't fit. The old dress looks ridiculous. The pant legs on your jeans seem to have shrunk up toward your knees.

Choices grow on us, too. They pile up, almost unnoticed, until one day they add up to something. And what they add up to is yourself—yourself with your own capacities, your own vices and virtues, your own history. Camus says somewhere that "after forty your face is your own responsibility." I'd alter that a little: much earlier on, perhaps already, your *self* is your own responsibility. Oh, there are givens. Biology and genetics give us the material for all that we choose. Accidents of birth and advantage—or disadvantage—will shape us somewhat. But above all, as human beings, we shape ourselves, and we do it in the choices we make.

In the spring of your senior year you choose a college. It probably seems to you one of the biggest and hardest choices you ever made. It must have been at once an exhilarating and an excruciating choice. But now I want to let you in on a secret: where you go to college is just the first of many choices, like my grandfather's choice of port from which to board ship. Any college is just a port of departure.

While you're at college you'll choose courses and majors and activities from a much bigger array than you've ever seen before. These are real choices—and important ones. But the college catalogue, again, isn't half so important a catalogue of choices as something else you'll barely notice. It's the catalogue of unwritten choices: who will your friends be, will they all be like yourself, or will you stretch to include people from different places and races with different ways of life, different ideas, people who will challenge you and push you. The freedom of these coming years, of this passage to adulthood, is a freedom to know and like or dislike a world's worth of people and activities. You will *have* to choose, and you *will* choose, even if you scarcely notice the choices you make.

Colleges can't choose for you. No one can. Good colleges, or good secondary schools, bring together lots of different people. But *you* will make the choices, and you will act on them. One of the small freedoms you will enjoy is the freedom to *leave* campus—to meet people at work or study, back and forth every day in community work, as a volunteer or intern, or away for a whole semester or year. Push yourself to try what's new, what's hard, what's different. Reach out to as many different people as you can. Try them. Talk to them. Argue with them. Listen to them. "Experience to me," says Emily Dickinson, "is everyone I meet."

All of this I can urge on you with a kind of joy. Try the roller coaster. See what ups and downs and turns it makes. You'll never get as good a chance again. But there are much graver, quieter choices to be made in these years. And let me say something of them before I'm done. "Experiment" is a word I use with ambivalence in this age of the bargain and the gamble. "Try it, you'll like it" is something people say in a thousand contexts, most of them innocent. Try this dance, this yogurt, this book, this class, this haircut; and so we do. We try hundreds of things. And I suppose that it's better to live in the spirit of trying things out than in the spirit of avoidance and timidity. But I said before that choices pile up on you. Janis Joplin is wrong. Freedom is *not* "just another word for nothing left to do." Freedom makes something: it makes lives and characters. In freedom we forge ourselves. Choices, trying things out, can sometimes trap you in a self that none of you would choose freely and knowingly.

Take alcohol. Many of you have tried it, in one form or another. Some of you may have already tried it to the point of real stupidity. Well, let me be frank. One of the choices young people everywhere are making is the choice to get drunk. Beer is the drug that plagues our campuses, not the cocaine and crack that plague our cities. And when I ask students: "Why do you drink so much? Why do you go out and get drunk?" the answer is, inevitably: "For the fun of it." "We're just having a good time." But there's more to it than a good time; they know it and I know it. There's the need, in the midst of the intense self-consciousness that afflicts us all in late adolescence, to let down your hair, to forget yourself—your scared, shy self—if only for an hour or two, and if only with a little something to loosen things up. I can see that. It's not the end of the world. But it is the beginning of an identity. And the person who chooses to get drunk for the fun of it, at nineteen, will be tempted in the sadness of inevitable defeats later on—and defeat *is* inevitable, sooner or later—that person at twenty nine or thirty nine, forty nine or fifty nine, will be tempted to choose it again, and again. Just as your bodies grew up when you were looking the other way, so will your habits, your lifelong character.

The simple point that I want to make to you is this: you will choose your self, your lifelong self, in all the small choices you make when you are at your freest. And the self you choose will itself never be so free, so up for grabs, as in these few years of experiment and exploration.

The choices you make about how to use your bodies and your brains, your sexuality and creativity, your energy and discipline, these choices add up. Make them with all the care and deliberation you can muster. Make them choices that will last, choices that will bring you joy. Make choices that make sense for you and for everyone around you.

Choose well.

GOING TO COLLEGE

Readiness

When I was in kindergarten and first grade, I went to a white clapboard school high on a hill. I don't remember what I learned there. I can remember the war games we fought on the playground. And I remember, most of all, two teachers and a principal who held conversations with my parents about when I might be "ready to learn to read." These conversations were always hushed and unclear to me, although the words "ready to learn" recurred again and again, in disappointment and with a faint note of exasperation. Because I was not ready to read I was not taught to read. So as a dutiful boy, I did not read.

This worried my parents but was fine with me. I had a seat in the back of the room among the more vigorous playground warriors. I found that the days passed happily. For me and my cohort, time in class served as a respite from battle. We whispered back and forth about the strategies we would deploy at the next recess.

I have always liked the notion of readiness to learn. It was responsible, I think, for the voracity of my reading habits once they took hold. The summer between first and second grade was one long tutorial, as my mother, who decided that I was ready to learn to read after all, set me to reading street signs and cereal boxes and the ingredients in various soups—a great and interesting if still somewhat neglected literature.

I come before you today to say in no uncertain or hushed tones: you are ready to learn. We have gathered you from around the country and around the world, with thousands of interests and skills. We gathered you because we judged that you would be the readiest learners we could find. And here at last, after endless discussion and deliberation, visits hither and yon, encouragements and hesitations, here at last is *your* college, the one you have chosen (and the one that has chosen you).

I want to say something to you about what college offers you—and, while you are listening, what you offer your college. What I have to say touches on a readiness deeper and more important than the one my first-grade teacher had in mind for me.

First, and most important, college offers you the liberal arts, unalloyed and undiluted. We borrow the term "liberal arts" from classical Rome.

By "liberal" we mean quite literally freeing or liberating.

All of you have felt in your lives the exhilaration of learning something, especially something difficult, as I did in that first summer of learning to read.

I remember still how clever I felt as I shouted out "Speed Limit 25" as my mother drove by signs on the road, slowly at first and then faster and faster as I learned to read the signs at a glance. By the end of that summer she was whizzing by at speeds much greater than the ones the signs suggested. It was not just cleverness that I felt, but something more powerful, more liberating. It was mastery, I think: the mastery of a whole world of words written down—speed limits, ingredients and instructions, Shakespeare.

All learning liberates: it frees us from ignorance; it frees us to accomplishment and to confidence. But the liberal arts share this ambition to liberate in a particular way. For the disciplines that make up the liberal arts—from physics to classics, from sculpture and painting to sociology and anthropology— are the hardest and broadest studies that we can pursue. These disciplines are those that have seemed to scholars here and on faculties around the world the most important sources of knowledge available to us.

What is justice? Why do we consider one painting or concerto beautiful and another merely competent? What is the most basic form of energy, and how can we observe and measure it? We never finish with such questions. They, more than any answer, *are* the liberal arts. They draw on us to understand the power of the human mind at work and at play in the world.

But why, you may ask, should we study subjects, however challenging and rigorous, that do not have a more practical application? Why the liberal arts rather than some more illiberal and practical art?

This is an important question, and practical is an important adjective within it. It comes from the Greek *praxis,* for action. The import of the question is that these subjects have no relation to action, to work and careers. Your parents may wonder why you are studying moral philosophy or political theory rather than something that will land you a job, and preferably as close on the heels of graduation as possible. It's tough finding a job as a practicing philosopher or poet, I admit. And your parents may not be so far off the mark in wondering what will become of you when you are done with school and trying to rely on your own efforts rather than theirs for material support.

But I hope they know—and I expect you do already—that there is a higher practicality that suggests that the liberal arts *are* the most practical—because the most powerful—subjects of study. They teach us not just about getting a job but about living, about creating jobs for others, and about our most fundamental purposes.

The readiness we see in you tells us that you are ready to learn more than you have ever learned before, both practically *and* theoretically.

Your readiness for this will require you to resist the temptation to study something because of what I will call its lower practicality—because it will help in a first job interview or in getting your first promotion or raise. Make the skills you acquire here be lifelong skills, useful not just at first, but at last.

This leads me to the second point I want to make about you and college, and your readiness for each other. Whether you knew it or not, you chose this college because of its teachers, because of what they know and how they teach. At the very center of the liberal arts tradition is discussion, conversation. Teaching and learning by conversation is what a good college prides itself on. This means many practical things: small classes, for one, arguments late into the night, for another. But, above all, it means a willingness to test ideas by trying them out, in the manner of a laboratory experiment. A college is a kind of laboratory of ideas, in the classroom and out, on the school paper, in community outreach, in sports teams, in the arts, even in politics.

A readiness to learn implies a readiness to try out ideas, even—or especially—unfamiliar ideas. You will learn more, and you will learn better, if you push yourself to learn what you have never learned before.

This means trying on ideas and experiences that will seem at first quite foreign. You will be tempted to take only those subjects that you already know you are good at. Resist that temptation. It is a form of timidity, or fear, and we all recognize its power to prevent us from learning.

There is a third point that I should make, and implicit in it is a caution. College will be a kind of freedom time for you. So much that was fixed before in your lives will seem now unfixed, open, up for grabs. You will face an exhilarating array of choices. Will I be an archeologist or a financier? Will I make friends with this strange but interesting person? Will I get up for breakfast?

There is a danger in so much freedom of drifting aimlessly, like a dilettante, or, on the other hand, of going off in directions that betray what you stand for. I urge you to experiment, to venture out, to risk both a little and a lot. But never, ever leave your good sense and moral judgment far behind. These are guides you will need now as never before.

Finally, I want you to know that any school or college is a kind of village.

This particular village is an enormously flexible and open one. Colleges have requirements, as you will soon learn. But the intellectual excitement in a college curriculum is that it is nearly always open to you to shape your own course of study. It will often be interdisciplinary study; that is the liberal arts heritage. It will engage the wide world around us; that is one of its glories. And always it will offer the guidance of experts whose vocation it is to teach. Discussions in this village will go on in class and out, from one week to the next, over the course of a semester, a year—a lifetime.

As you begin today, I want you to think, if only for a moment, about your own effect on the college, your own part in this village of the liberal arts.

Someday, years from now, you will look back on this choice, this college, and say: "I went there." May there be pride for you in that short sentence, and joy, and a sense that you made the most of it.

Beginnings

In one very particular sense, I wasn't ready for college. I was only going a half hour from home. That gave me the luxury of having to make only a few travel arrangements to get there. Unfortunately, I made none. When the day came, I started out at the last possible moment, borrowing my father's car, stuffing my clothes into my old Boy Scout duffel bag. As I drove into town, feeling very grown up in my borrowed car, I leaned out the window to wave to a high-school friend trudging down the sidewalk. He saw me and waved back, but I didn't see that the car was getting mighty close to the truck stopped ahead of me and that I hadn't braked hard enough to bring the car to a full stop. *Bang*, went the front end as I smashed the headlight into the back of the truck's platform. I looked over, and my friend laughed and trudged on.

This is the first day of what will take you four years to complete. You will have a collision or two along the way; you will have friends; you will make it, one way or another. What's it all about?

Sometimes, in our strategic plans for a college, we ask ourselves this question in an altered form. What do we as educators hope to achieve by all that we do? We want to graduate educated women and men, we say, liberally educated, educated in the liberal arts. These are the studies that have proven the most fruitful and the most enduring. We want you to study hard, to go into a broad array of subjects, and to study one or two in depth. We make a special effort to study across disciplines, in those areas where disciplines intersect. But we want you to do much more than study. We want you to make friends, to participate in community work, in the arts, in sports and student government, we want you to engage the wider world represented by this city, its people and institutions; we want you to travel and explore.

We want you to do all of these things, but we want you to do one additional thing that is both more and less than the sum of these. We want you to find in yourself, through these studies and experiences, through the risks you take and the challenges you overcome, a growing sense of responsibility—for yourself, for those you care about, and for the world as you will live in it, know it, and shape it. That sense of responsibility has its foundation in both freedom and understanding. Let me say something about each of them.

Coming to college is coming into a freedom time in your own lives. You can sense that, I am sure. Nervous or even bewildered as you may be this afternoon, you must also feel the exhilaration that comes with going away to college. You leave behind not only the immediate supervision of parents and schools but also the fixed routines and settled expectations of your place among your friends, many of whom may have known you since you were a child.

Break free while you are here. Decide who you want to be, and then go for it. If you have a yen to try painting or acting, the school paper, or a sport you have never tried, do it. If you hung out with a certain crowd before, try to make friends who are different from you and can surprise you and challenge you. Don't be like the tourist who travels a thousand miles from home only to seek out the nearest McDonald's and the other tourists from the same hometown.

Your studies are of a piece with your lives. Try what you haven't tried before. If you're sure of yourself in science or poetry, venture out into territory you haven't yet conquered. We'll push you to do it, but unless you get excited and do it on your own, we—and you—won't have accomplished much.

The point of all this is not the new and different for their own sake, or to keep you from being bored. The point is this: we don't believe in the *educated* person, but rather in the *educating,* the *self-educating* person, who is eager to learn, unfazed by the hard work of it, and both curious and confident about the powers of the mind. Neither our curiosity nor our confidence make us believe for a moment that there will always be answers to our questions (no more than we believe that every new acquaintance will mature into a firm friend).

There are mysteries in the world, and there are questions we cannot now answer.

The tradition of the liberal arts would have us love questions and the work of learning almost for their own sake. Do not get me wrong, though; there *are* answers. So much so that the joy of answering questions will stir in some of you a vocation as an artist, a scholar, an inventor. But there are not *always* going to be answers, not until we put an end to questions. Where there is no answer, there can still be understanding; and with it a lessening of fear and, often, the quelling of rash opinion or prejudice.

This leads me back to responsibility. You cannot take responsibility, even for your own actions, unless you feel that you have a choice in the matter. Choice requires freedom. But you cannot make much of freedom—of unhindered choice—unless you understand the context and consequences of your actions (and of the actions of others, as well).

You chose a particular college in a particular place; and that college chose you from among many applicants. These were good choices, likely as not.

For us, the choice was not just of a class drawn from around the country and around the world; it was not just a choice of your good scores and your good grades, of your leadership in activities or your special gifts as actors and musicians, entrepreneurs and poets. It was a choice of who this college would become.

Your class, drawn from most of the states and from many other countries, from every conceivable background, rich and poor, rural and urban, brings to intelligence, energy, and a wide range of enthusiasms. The person who worked so hard for Habitat for Humanity will join the field hockey star in a seminar on Asian religions; the singer who has soloed many times will be in a production with someone who has never performed before; next to you in chem lab will be one person who has already done original research and another whose gifts for the subject are just becoming apparent.

The faculty, too, chose the college. Ask them why. Virtually without exception, they chose it because of you and your predecessors and successors. They wanted to teach, and they wanted to teach in a setting in which bright students pursue rigorous studies side by side with processors working on original projects of their own. By the time you are juniors and seniors, with traditional or interdisciplinary majors of your own, many of you will take up research or writing or artistic projects in collaboration with your professors. You will have taken charge of your own learning, and in doing so you will have stepped up to the responsibility of teaching others about the path of a virus, the history of the federal deficit, the growth of our cities and suburbs, about Russian painting or the lives of children in Eastern Europe or here at home.

In the next several years you will see many changes, in yourself and in the college. Our changes will be designed to make our teaching and your learning more successful. We hope to make better use of this place, a microcosm of the challenges America will face in your lifetime. Among these are the challenges of making government work better, of adapting our businesses to international markets, and, perhaps above all, of redeeming the promise of America for *all* of our people.

Your education on this campus—this home base from which to launch your studies and adventures in these freest years of your lives—your education here should prepare you to live the rest of your life in the spirit of the liberal arts. It is a spirit that is at once serious and joyful, curious and eager, open to challenge, ready to meet the world and to engage with its people.

At the end of each academic year, before the processional at graduation, I give a charge—a direction—to the senior class as its members hurry off toward lives beyond campus. College presidents are kept around for just such moments, you see. Then with deep voices and rounded phrases, dressed in medieval paraphernalia, they risk making fools of themselves in an attempt to give one last drop of wisdom to students whose chief thought, at the end of a hot afternoon, may well be "Please, be brief."

Better to give you the charge today. You are just beginning. You are likely to listen a bit more closely. And you and I will be seeing a lot of one another, talking over these ideas, in the next four years or so.

Here, then, is my charge to you as you begin:

You will be lonely sometimes. Accept that as a given. Loneliness is the price you pay for taking a risk, for trying something others have not tried, for being yourself.

Take this freedom that is yours for these few years and embrace it; you will never see its like again.

Study hard, but study playfully as well. Let your imagination and your sense of humor run free in these years on this campus. Study is work—all learning is—but it can be, it should be, joyful work.

Take up ownership here—of your own studies, of your friendships, of your dormitory life, of your successes and your failures. The college is yours. It is your responsibility to make something of it.

And finally, whatever happens in the next four years, you will leave something of yourself behind. Years from now, when the question comes up of your own autobiography, you will say: "And then I went to college. . . ." Let the story you tell then be a good one, of friendships, of poems and paintings, experiments and adventures, debates with faculty and late-night bull sessions in the dorms. Tell how you learned more about yourself, what strengths you had, what gifts you brought to college and what gifts were awakened here. Tell what discoveries you made, what risks you took. Most of all, tell those who ask that you made the best of a rare freedom.

Ambition

Nearly twenty years ago my father was very sick. He had been hospitalized at Yale–New Haven Hospital in Connecticut. He and my mother lived in the house where I grew up, down along the shore toward New York City, about a half hour away by car. I must have been back there with my own family visiting in the early summer or late spring, around this time of year. Someone needed to go up to the hospital to bring him home. I volunteered: it would be a chance to spend some time with him and a chance too to drive his cherished sports car, a Mercedes 450SL.

When I checked him out of the hospital I asked if we could take a longer route home. Maybe I mentioned the shore roads. We ended up meandering along Route 1 on a succession of half loops to various beach towns between New Haven and Fairfield. The beach along Long Island Sound is nothing to make postcards of: there are a lot of small houses, some run-down bars, a few pretty piers and old Victorian neighborhoods. The Sound isn't the ocean, it's a big salty pond, murky with all the rivers—including the Connecticut—that silt into it. But it's familiar water to me and was to my father. He had grown up on one of those rivers, and I had grown up along the shore.

Not far from New Haven—in a little town called Milford—he said that he recognized some of the shore houses and a little park. "We used to come down here before the Depression," he said. "We rented one of these places." He pointed to a bunch of ramshackle cottages at a more or less defunct motel. I asked him what it was like then, coming down in an old Ford they had: he and his brothers and his parents, renting some rooms, dispersing along the little patches of gray beach, swimming and playing ball. I can remember his gaunt smile and his unshaven jaw as he recalled it all. He was one of nine brothers, and there was lots of daring and who-goes-first and who-can-climb-higher among them.

As we were leaving town I asked him if he played only with his brothers in those days. "No, there were friends down at the same time," he told me. "Who?" I asked. He recalled two or three names. One, in particular, brought back memories of long swims out to a buoy in the Sound at night. "What ever became of him?" I asked. He laughed a little. "I don't know exactly. Last I heard he had moved out to California and was sort of a beach bum." We both liked this idea and chuckled together at the thought that someone my father's age—just about seventy—had held out all those years against the expectations of a career and success, against fame or wealth or good works. I had the sense that my father's laughter harbored a judgment that it was a silly way to live your life. "Dad, do you think he was as happy as the guys like you with careers?" I said. He mused a bit on the young man he remembered. "Maybe he was," he said.

I don't know how many of you are headed for the nearest or farthest beach soon. And if you get there I don't know how long you will stay. But I suspect that a few of you are still puzzling hard over where to head out from here. Your parents may have all sorts of ideas about your future; your friends must have notions; you may even have a job starting this fall or a graduate school to go to. But I mean something much more general: your direction in life. The question is not "Where will you be in September?" but "Where are you headed in life?" What do you want to make of yourself? What do you want to do with your life? What are your ambitions?

Ambition was not always the good thing that your parents and friends may tell you. Only since the last century has the term shaken off its origins among the deadly sins to take on the obligatory cast that it now assumes. "Did this in Caesar seem ambitious?" Marc Antony asked in Shakespeare. Did it seem, in other words, excessive, prideful, domineering? We have tamed the term now and, particularly among the young, hold it out as a sort of extracurricular requirement. "Be ambitious"; meaning, be successful, powerful, famous, maybe rich. And some of you—many of you—are ambitious. But for what, exactly?

Many, many centuries ago, Socrates was criticized sharply for bothering his fellow Athenians with unanswerable questions about what they wanted from life and how they went about seeking it. Let me bother you, then, Socratically, with some questions about the ambition that thrusts you forward toward the rest of your lives.

Ambition seems to come in two forms: there is the desire, first, to pass your time doing something—teaching, painting, doing medicine, starting a business, caring for kids. It's a way of saying: "I like doing this and I want to go on doing it for much of my life." But I would guess that only a handful of you have already formed a definite ambition in this sense. Most of the rest of you might wonder what sorts of things you'd like to do, what sorts of things would make you contented or fulfilled, but I doubt that you have figured out an answer to the question: is there one thing you'd like to work at from here on in? When you can answer the question you will have come to feel a vocation, a calling. "This is it; this is what I want to do; nothing else quite satisfies me; this is the work I want to do." A calling is something like falling in love: "This is the one I want to spend my life with," you will say. It's a wonderful feeling and, I hope, a lasting one. But more than a feeling, a vocation is a compass for your energy and drive. It can guide you through many a challenge and perplexity.

Anyone who has ever worked with a craftsman in one of the less celebrated or gloried professions—a gardener, say, or a carpenter—has felt some of the modesty and devotion in achievement that comes with a sense of vocation, with a calling. The good gardener glories in her garden, takes pride in it, and often smiles at a compliment or the delight of passersby.

The vision of the garden is only the beginning. It is necessarily followed by days or months or years of work, of digging and planting, weeding and watering—and seasons of hopeful, attentive waiting. But then, as if by magic, the garden is suddenly and gloriously in full bloom—the colors of the petals, the soft early green of the new leaves, the crowded jostling of the plants one against another. The gardener achieves a quiet ambition in a quiet way.

The gardens of our backyards are mostly ambitions writ small. French moralists like Voltaire and Montaigne always turn to the garden to symbolize their rejection of the larger world and its vanities. But now I want to put to you the case of a gardener dissatisfied with these quiet satisfactions: what about the gardener who wants to be rich and powerful—and recognized as the greatest of them all? What's wrong with that? There has to be a relationship somewhere between the backyard garden or pond and the immense gardens of Kyoto or Versailles or Central Park.

And here we come to the second sort of ambition, the fiercer sort. This is the ambition we hear so much of in Shakespeare, the headstrong drive toward ends with names like glory or fame, wealth, power, success. I would guess that most of you feel this ambition, but perhaps still as a somewhat unfocused desire for these things in your life, someday, somehow.

"Fling [it] away," Shakespeare counseled, "by that sinne fell the angels." But to fling away ambition may be neither good—nor possible.

Assume for a moment that no one had any ambition for these things, that no one wanted fame or glory. We would be left with a world in which some or all of us acquired vocations for certain arts and achievements, and exercised these vocations for the sheer joy of them: art for art's sake, the gentler ambitions of vocation in charge of all our works and days. There would be a wonderful unselfishness in that utopia, a modesty in achievement that might seem rare today.

But would we have a world as rich in science and art and commerce and education as the one you have grown up in? There is no way to know for sure. My own hunch is that we would not. Let me give two examples. I have had good reason in my own life to give thanks for medicine. Yet I have certainly seen the competitiveness and arrogance that often accompany great skill and learning in subjects like surgery and oncology. The rivalries of medical scientists are legend. Surely these rivalries and ambitions account for some portion of the discovery and learning that heal us.

Take the liberal arts as another example. Anthony Trollope once said that he saw no reason to write novels except for money—and he might have added fame. Most of us don't like to hear that works of art come from such a measly desire as extra cash. Are poems and plays and books and buildings all the products of a kind of vanity, a desire, that is, for one person to grow rich and famous, to bask in applause and smiles and a kind of pagan worship? The lack of ambition—of a desire for glory, wealth, power—would rob us all of many of the works that we study together.

All of you at one time or another have felt the giddy sensation that you'd not only survive the transition from childhood to adulthood—but that you'd ace it. You'd end up rich and famous and living in Manhattan or Malibu with throngs knocking at your door. But at college, as you got a little closer to the fantasy, you came across a counter to all this: you have to sell out to get rich and maybe to get famous. You have to sell out something or other to be powerful. Is it worth it? Is it ever worth it?

That depends on what we mean by selling out.

To most of us, the phrase evokes a very primitive barter in which we take what we most value in ourselves—whatever it is—and trade it for something that we want, but shamefully or guiltily.

In one of the most elaborate fables of ambition ever written, Charles Dickens wrote of the boy he called Pip. Born an orphan in the desolate marsh country in the west of England, Pip is raised by an older sister and her wonderful blacksmith husband, Joe Gargery, Pip's truest friend. Soon Pip learns that he has a great but mysterious expectation of wealth and prominence. An unknown benefactor has settled a fortune on him for reasons he cannot fathom. The novel tells a convoluted tale of the boy's quest—through treachery and danger—to reach these great expectations and to take his high place in British society. Only at the very end does a chastened Pip realize that his expectations (and even his life) were watched over all the while by the poor people he wanted so desperately to leave behind in his ambition for greatness.

Rarely if ever do we go quite so far astray as Pip; rarely will we all come back home in the end as he does. Dickens was writing a fable, with fabulous adventures and a fabulous conclusion. But the lesson of the fable holds.

Dickens' lesson is not that ambition is wrong, in Pip's life or his own. It is the subtler lesson that ambition must be disciplined over and again by a sense of what we care most about as we go about our lives amid complexity and confusion.

Ambition is a passion. Like any passion—jealousy, love, hatred—it can make you its tool. It can take over and drive everything else before it, sometimes destroying those whom you love along the way.

Like Pip, most of you will not escape life's exhilarating temptations. Money matters; only a few of you will be able to live as if it does not. Power matters, too, if more subtly. And fame or celebrity will tug at you as well, whether you seek them or not. All of these are forms of power, I think, types of command or influence over the attention of others. Hegel once said that above all we seek recognition by others. He was not far off the mark.

My hunch is that you too will want these things. You may not; you may reject them; but most of you will have to contend with ambition—with the need in yourselves for power and acclaim—as much as with hunger and desires of all kinds.

Ultimately, the question of ambition is a question about what you want from life and from yourself. The Stoics thought they had a way out by distinguishing sharply between the things you can control in your life and things you cannot. Their lesson was to confine your ambitions to the things you control.

But life does not lend itself to strict control. Things will surprise you and baffle you, things in you and things in others. Ambition is an inescapable energy in your lives, a striving for more and better, an effort to prove yourself against others.

Here then is the simplest lesson I can give you on this subject: let your ruling ambition be your ambition to have a craft, a discipline that you cherish and follow as your own. Treat the wilder, fiercer forms of ambition within you as real and powerful. Accept them and use them. But always keep them in harness to your ideals of a life well lived. There is no more desperately unhappy man or woman than the one who chases down great possessions or great victories, great achievements, while losing hold of the person he or she always wanted to be.

Serious Play

"Beginnings are always hard," says the Talmud. They should be hard; they should be hard enough to demand your best effort even amid discouragement. But they should never make you despair or lose your way.

You begin today your studies. I want to ask the question Why here? The college recruited you, of course, so that it might be fair for you to ask *me* to answer that question. And I want to try to answer it for you, for myself, and for many others who wonder what defines us now and what will define us in the future.

Forgive me if I am a little personal in what I say. Someone once said that college presidents have only two important tasks, balancing the budget and articulating a vision of what we're about. I spend much of my time speaking to alumni, to parents, to faculty and others about our common concerns. Today let me speak to students. What vision do those of us on the faculty and staff have of your education here, your choice to come to college here?*

*Trinity College.

Each of us takes on this question in a somewhat different spirit, with a little different turn and emphasis, like a painter mixing colors on a palette.

The first time I visited the college was years ago, in February. The days were short, and I had arrived at the airport near dusk. By the time I had rented a car and found my way here—using the Admissions Office directions, as you and your parents did—it was dark. I forget where I parked; there were plenty of spaces; the campus seemed a little deserted, and was. It was the end of Open Period, the week of independent study that we instituted several years ago, toward the end of which upperclass students often take off for the hills. The temperature was falling quickly, and my raincoat was hardly a match for a snow squall that was festering. I found my way to the dining hall and paid a lordly visitor's $6.50 for a supper of lasagna. I sat down with four juniors. Without saying why I was there—interviewing—I asked what they thought of the place. "We work hard; we play hard," one of them said, in a phrase I have heard over and over since then.

In a sense, it's the undergraduate ideal. I accept it as such and, though these are not my own terms, I will try to explore them here with you, since they may soon be *your* terms. We begin with a simple relation, teaching: someone who knows a little more trying to help someone who knows a little less learn—about a subject, a technique, a place, a language, a culture. This college is built around teaching. It is the reason we are here and the reason behind virtually all that we do, our athletics, our entertainments, our research.

Any school can say the same, you may object. A school is a place of teaching and learning. But here, as among a small circle of liberal arts colleges, almost all of them in America, our approach to teaching is guided by two strong principles: first, we believe that the best teaching is a kind of conversation. This means that we teach in settings intimate enough for conversation, for discussion, in all our departments and at all levels. It is a cause for embarrassment here—and perhaps should be—when the popularity of a course brings enrollments of eighty or a hundred. It also means that the teaching relation here is one between professor and student, not student and graduate student or student and teaching assistant. Martin Buber, the great rabbinical theologian, spoke of the relation between us and God as an "I/Thou" relation, one in which we know each other intimately, personally. Teaching here is an I/Thou relation, certainly not to a god, but to someone learned, expert, in a field.

This leads me to the second strong principle, a principle governing the fields we study. We study and teach the liberal arts, the freeing arts. Here we must all countenance some ambiguity in our definition. Which among all the fields of study are "freeing" in this sense? I cannot fix them for you, once and for all, in an exact definition. They form a tradition, and like any good tradition, one that has some sparkle and life in it, one that renews itself.

Any study will reward discipline and reflection with insight and even wisdom. A school for pickpockets, like Fagin's in Dickens' *Oliver Twist,* no doubt teaches remarkable things about human behavior and culture, about physics and economics. It may even, in its way, teach about morality. Or, to take more innocent examples, the study of marketing and advertising—two of the most popular undergraduate majors in this country—will reward some who study in these fields with more than the proficiencies advertised under these labels. They will learn, that is, not just the rudiments of these useful and profitable arts, not just what they need to get and hold a job in these fields, they will also learn, perhaps, more basic skills in writing and analysis, and discover something of art or literature. But if they do venture in this way through these disciplines to larger questions and skills, they do so not so much by design as by chance, or by the inevitable connection among all the threads of learning.

We set out on a different path in the liberal arts. We study, as Cardinal Newman once wrote, not for *usefulness*, or at least not for an immediate and practical usefulness. We study to free ourselves. The usefulness, then, the *use* of these liberal arts, lies in preparing the way for that freedom that is their ideal.

It goes almost without saying that it is a freedom *through* understanding or knowledge. The question that answers your wonder about which subjects to include within the liberal arts is what subjects will teach us the most about freeing ourselves—inwardly and in our relations to others and to the world.

These two principles—of teaching in a face-to-face conversation between professor and student and of our commitment to studies in the liberal arts—structure our every effort as a college. Whether or not you would state it in this way, I am convinced that most of you came here because you believed that this was the kind of institution you wanted.

These commitments lend continuity as well as conviction to all that we do. The most challenging or radical questions about science or politics or art should be part of the liberal arts tradition because it is a tradition that seeks to liberate or free. And freedom's first requirement is that we put aside fear. Our tradition renews itself by asking difficult, sometimes troubling questions. If we fear these questions, or the answers we may arrive at, then we cannot inquire except halfheartedly or timidly. There may be right answers and wrong answers, correct and incorrect answers. What there is not, what there cannot be, in our tradition, is correctness or conformity in the sorts of things you should wonder and inquire about, or the sorts of answers you can conceive. This means that if the question is—as it is for some—whether the tradition of the liberal arts is itself stifling or repressive, then we will not shy from that question either, lest we shy from the goal we set ourselves.

Three other features of our tradition need to be stated. All will, in one way or another, have entered into your decision. The first is the wholeness, the completeness of the educational effort in the liberal arts tradition. Athletics, student government, arts productions, the residence halls, community work: we would hope that students would participate in the broadest range of activities, testing and pushing themselves in and out of the classroom.

The freedom that comes through knowledge must find expression in every portion of your life. While you are here, as an undergraduate, you will have a chance to work at studies, at sports, at politics, even at romance. If "work hard, play hard" can mean to you that you throw your passions into the theater, the radio station, a tutoring project, a poem, then I take the motto as my own. It is part of my vision of what college permits. In a world whose sheer scale of numbers will soon require of you great focus and specialization, this scale will permit you a voyage in which you try on more than one work, more than one possible self. This play—deep, serious play— is the work of freeing all of your capacities.

The second feature of our tradition that I must say something about is our setting.* We are unusual as a liberal arts college in finding ourselves in an inner-city neighborhood. We embrace the city, not because we are a college of social work or urban policy or because we believe we can save America's cities. We are not and cannot; we remain a college of liberal arts, where ancient Greece or modern Tibet, the cell of mitochondria or the theory of numbers can hold our attention as much as city school systems or housing for the homeless. But the difficulties—and the joys—of America's cities are an especially important subject for reflection and study in the liberal arts. If our political and constitutional system is, as I believe, one of America's great achievements, then its failure to integrate city and suburb, rich and poor, black and white, stands as a great contradiction of the astonishingly durable virtues of its constitutional order. At a time when the world as a whole seems particularly eager to have free markets and free politics, America's failings in its cities sober our enthusiasm and test both our resolve and our wisdom.

While you are here, get to know the city and its people. Work as a tutor; walk through downtown and its neighborhoods; go to the movies and a restaurant. "I have traveled a great deal lately," wrote Henry David Thoreau at a time in his life when he hardly set foot outside the little township of Concord, Massachusetts. You, too, should travel a good deal hereabouts, travel imaginatively and intellectually. The city gives a unique if sometimes daunting course in the human condition and its social and political contradictions.

Finally, I want to say something about the curriculum, that great gatherer of students and teachers, of research and curiosity, of experiment and tradition. Each college or university takes a stand with a curriculum, a stand that tells of the convictions of its faculty about what the liberal arts are, and about what you, our students, should try your minds at. Two principles go to the heart of the liberal arts curriculum. Those are, first, tolerance for all points of view, and, second, balance in the interplay between tradition and innovation. Both principles hold today in any good curriculum and on any good faculty.

There is always a pull in a college or university between freedom and constraint. Or, to put this more personally, a pull between studying *what* you choose and *as* you choose and studying with the guidance of a syllabus or a curriculum, under the direction of a skilled and learned teacher. You may want to study what you like and nothing besides. A teacher may feel that you will take the most intellectual profit from a highly structured sequence of courses. Trinity has experimented—and experiments still—with the right balance between these impulses or desires.

A curriculum is never finished because, ultimately, a curriculum is about the world. And if by the world we mean all the world, all that we can imagine and know, then there is always more to it, defying us to study and learn, to master and create. We are never done with change and with the difficulties of understanding it. As you make your way through the college's curriculum, know that what we seek for you and with you is your freedom, through knowledge and mastery. Challenge the curriculum, challenge us, your faculty. Recognize at the same time what we seek in pushing you to work hard with us and with the ideas that are the tools of our trade—and yours.

Those of us who have come to love a college, and to give it our labor of love, believe that here you will find an education that matches any in the world. To have such an education is a privilege, but one that must be earned. Late nights with your eyes reddened by long, hard reading; hourly returns to the lab to make sure your experiment is in good order; painful criticism of your painting or your song by classmates or a teacher—this is some of the hard work of learning. Aristotle said that learning is an unlimited good because there is no end to it. To say that it is hard work is not to take away its joy. Among the small lessons you must soon learn is that you cannot have great joy without great labor. And few of us will devote great labor without great love.

A college is the work of the many who have loved it, first as an idea—a college truly tolerant of all views—and then as an institution, often an old institution. Its commitments to the liberal arts and to teaching as a conversation will hold up, not just through its second century but much beyond. Today you join a tradition that will change you, and that you will change. Work hard in that tradition; play hard in it; learn the rigors and the joys of study in these liberal arts of ours. In choosing a college you have chosen more than you knew. Good luck in your choice.

THE COLLEGE COMMUNITY

Roommates

I had three roommates my freshman year. On the first or second day they agreed that I was in big trouble. They had interrogated me and found that in addition to other oddities of character, I had some strange convictions that might endanger my health and happiness (or even theirs): I intended to avoid all college "mixers"; I did not drink or smoke; I hoped as soon as possible to take part in a social revolution; and, most curious of all, I was found out as a churchgoer more than once a week. None of them accepted the argument that I liked my life as it was. They emphatically rejected the tolerant wisdom of live and let live. "No, no," they chortled, "we've got to turn you around—and fast." "Give me one month," said Felix, in his formal British way. "Do as I do for one single month and you will learn the error of your ways. You're missing out on all that makes life worthwhile."

"Nah, Felix, it's not that easy," said Wendell, "Gerety's been this way for a while now. Let's take a year and do it right. We'll take him to mixers; we'll force him to drink; we'll make him skip church. By the end of the year he'll be almost normal."

This was thirty-some years ago. I never did make it to a mixer or smoke much of anything; I tried revolution but didn't get far; and my Puritan views have slackened a bit, I admit.

When I first got the notice of who my roommates would be I felt terribly let down. This was in the summer of 1964. I was coming back from Paris. I don't know what I imagined, but I remember asking for "people different from me" on the form for roommate preferences—the form that asks about smoking, staying up late, noise-making, and so on. All of us, I learned, had gone to boarding schools. This suggested to me that we would all be the same in some important way. It didn't quite turn out that way.

I came the shortest distance, so, predictably, I got there last and got the last assignment. There were two singles across an open hallway: they went to the early arrivals. Wendell was from Michigan, and Kim was from New York City. Then there was a double with two beds. When I got there, one was already taken. Bags were strewn on the bed and on the floor; one of two dressers was taken. Hours later I met my roommate, Felix Downes-Thomas, from the Gambia, in West Africa. His mother ran a taxi service in Bathurst, the capital city (now called Banjul). "Gerety," he called me, in a deep African British voice. He and Wendell, across the hall, were a year or two older. I am in touch with both of them, one often, the other less so but with no less delight when we connect by letter or phone, in an airport or Grand Central Station. The third I have not seen since the year after graduation.

I want to put the simple question: What's so important about roommates? More generally and less metaphorically, what has residential life got to do with a college education? Were we stripping college down to its essentials, and building it up from the bottom, we would start, I take it, with teachers and students, a library, laboratories. Why not stop there? City College, in New York, joins the tradition of European universities that begin and end with these essentials. By residential life, I mean dormitories, a dining hall, fields and grounds, a gymnasium. Why do we need or want all that? Is it really helpful to us?

The question matters not because the economics of education forces us to consider a round of cutbacks; we're not at the point of selling off the Campus Center, or renting out the Chapel. The question matters because we—and by we I mean the family of colleges and universities in our tradition—we seem sometimes to have lost our way in residential life: we're no longer sure (if we ever were) of what our ends are in residential life, and less sure still of whether we're achieving them.

Whenever a college was founded in America, residence halls (and a house for the president) went up right away. The towns and villages were mostly small in the early days. The residence halls were necessary if more than a handful of students were to enroll in the new college. There was usually room for students, two or more to a room, with fireplaces but no other amenities. Each college had a president and two or three other faculty, all residing nearby, often within a field or two of the chapel. All over the country, colleges were founded with faculties, classrooms, a shelf or two of books, a microscope, a telescope—and residence halls. In a thinly populated country there was no alternative. Farm boys roomed with farm boys from distances that then seemed immense, though today we might cross them in an hour's drive or an hour's flight. Social life seems to have consisted of adolescent pranks and flirtation with young women from the villages and later the female seminaries.

"The students of Amherst in those early days," wrote William S. Tyler, an early historian of Amherst College, "were comparatively free from exciting and distracting circumstances. They came here to study, and they had nothing else to do."

Was there an ideal, or set of ideals, in these residential and dining arrangements? An echo of Oxford or Cambridge, or, more far fetched, of Plato's Academy and Aristotle's Lyceum? Not as far as anyone can tell. Monasteries might have seemed the nearest analogy to the fierce religious convictions of most of the early faculty—or perhaps Sparta's training camps for young soldiers. (Alumni, by the way, still speak fondly of the boot camp rigors of a generation back.)

By 1890, when Calvin Coolidge came down by train from Vermont, Amherst College was well established, with graduates in every field and a reputation for intellectual vigor. Coolidge got off at the station on Main Street and went looking for a boardinghouse, one run by a family friend, in fact. By this time the first of the dormitories were used almost exclusively for classes, laboratories, and study halls. Only a handful of students remained in residence on campus. The rest roomed and ate in town, occasionally with professors' families. Most students would join one of the newly fashionable Greek-letter societies. In a wealthier period, before Coolidge was long gone, the fraternities built the great houses that now make up perhaps half of our dormitories.

Coolidge started Amherst twice: the first time he dropped out on his second or third day; his father came down to retrieve his feverish son after one day of the notorious entrance exams in classics, history, and mathematics. His second start, a year later, went better. He took the exams, found a boardinghouse, and began classes. He wrote home that "college life . . . more than meets my expectations in the large amount of work required: I recite 16 hours a week besides chapel, lectures and gymnasium. . . ." As befitted a puritan and even Calvinist school, Amherst left no room for free choice in its curriculum. Even workouts at the gym were required, with showers or "sprays" part of the discipline.

Social life then *was* free; you were on your own as a student at college, fending for yourself in housing, meals, and entertainment. "I shall like [Amherst] better as I become better acquainted," Coolidge wrote his father at the outset. But the loneliness was not much disguised in the admission that "I don't seem to get acquainted very fast. . . ." He went to everything but participated little: in the fall there was a "cane rush" between the freshmen and sophomore classes, a brawl for the possession of a broomstick; Coolidge enjoyed watching his classmates in this struggle. He went to athletic events not only on campus but in Springfield, where Harvard and Yale played before thousands of students from around New England. "Tall, thin, somber, usually alone," Coolidge remained for nearly four years an outsider on campus, with very few friends. An *Ouden*—Greek for "not" or "nothing"—when it came to joining the fraternities, he was one of only a handful not asked to join during freshman year.

I bring up Coolidge not because of his later career but because of the vividness to me of his experience at Amherst as a student, and because of his loneliness. I should tell you that he managed before it was over to escape from the worst of the loneliness. His chance came in class when required to give a short speech. He amazed his classmates with the wit of what he had prepared and the confidence with which he spoke. In his senior year he was chosen to give the Grove Oration and to preside over various toasts at dinners and parties. That year he is said to have shot a college gardener in the seat of his pants with a Bee Bee gun. He blossomed senior year and even joined a fraternity.

Many find college lonely at first. Students everywhere complain of the lack of social life. A portion of that is a deeper complaint about how hard it is to connect with others and to make friends. It *is* hard, and, try as we may, we teachers and administrators cannot be of much help. You will see the residential system with its various services striving, not always successfully, to make college less lonely for you. No one in the nineteenth century would have seen it quite that way. Doc Hitchcock, who instituted physical education at Amherst, lectured Coolidge and others that "at bottom each one of us is solitary, alone with God. . . ."

It is a paradox of our age that you are at once much freer than your predecessors and much more fussed over; you may also be lonelier. In social life, the college can do little more than set the stage for your own efforts. Two of the most volatile issues in your personal lives—sexuality, and the use of alcohol or drugs—are at stake. We on the faculty and in the administration would be awkward tutors in the very personal choices you will make. We can give medical and psychological advice, and we can share what we know from our own experiences. Both literature and social science teach the lesson Doc Hitchcock taught. We cannot expel loneliness, and we cannot watch over you from morning until night.

THE COLLEGE COMMUNITY

Some historians of these institutions believe that the residential system is a remnant, a leftover, of our past, and that it serves no particular purpose. At first, we had no place to lodge the students in a small village: dormitories were necessary. Later on, when the village grew, we gave up the dormitories that we had. But then the fraternities stepped in, eventually building houses for many students. With the Second World War and later with coeducation, the student bodies grew again, to the point that colleges either needed to build dormitories or to return to the age of the boardinghouse. In the event, the colleges and universities built the dormitories they needed. We have been trying to make sense of them ever since.

This brief history suggests to some what one historian calls an accommodation[1]* with our past, rather than a coherent set of ideals or purposes for our future. Professor Frederick Rudolph argues that "the collegiate idea" can be a trap for a kind of rustic well-roundedness that often will not abide serious intellectual standards. "The notion," he writes, is that "a curriculum, a library, a faculty, and students are not enough to make a college." The "collegiate way" requires sports, dining halls, dormitories, and much else. But it is "permeated," he says, "by paternalism," by "hand-holding and spoon-feeding."[2]** It makes a college not so much an intellectual center as a special kind of late-adolescent retreat. As a Wellesley president once put it: "Merely for good times, for romance, for society, college life offers unequalled opportunities."[3]

The unequalled opportunity that I most remember from my own first months of college was the simple and obvious one of talk, of a particular kind of talk. It was sometimes with one other person, sometimes with three or four, almost never with many more. We were new to our setting and to one another; we were new to the freedoms of college and the peculiar mix of lenience and discipline that our studies permitted, or even required. We stayed up late; we crammed for exams and papers; we ate meals at strange

---

1. William S. Tyler, *A History of Amherst College* (New York: Frederick H. Hitchcock, 1895), p. 35.
2. Frederick Rudolph, *The American College and University* (New York: Vintage Books, 1962), p. 108.
3. Ibid., pp. 89–90.

hours; we washed only occasionally. Most of all, we talked. And most of our talk was, I am sure, of ourselves, although politics, novels, sex, science, and history all made their way into the conversation—often in the guise of grandiose schemes for our later lives.

As I reflect back on it now, the ideas ingredient in those conversations were nothing to write down for future generations. Like the talk of lovers, what we said enthralled us at the time because it was about us, about who we were, or more exactly who, briefly, passionately, we yearned to be. The unleashing of these yearnings—their articulation and exploration—was, for many of us, breathtaking, liberating. I suppose we felt liberated from childhood, from the oversight of parents, from the small choices of childhood toward the larger ones of adulthood. There was exaggeration in this, but it was a motivating and even inspiring exaggeration, one that would gradually draw us on to the balance of choice and acceptance that we all must find in our adult lives.

How can a college foster this sort of conversation? The best of it, for me, was probably after class, as one idea led to another and the themes of the lecture or seminar flowed into the themes and anxieties that were mine and my friends'. But if I had to choose the next most important contribution of college, it would be the meals. The commons—the tradition, that is, of meals in common—rivals the classroom as a setting for conversation. Amherst College's greatest lack in the time of Coolidge was a commons. And it was a lack that students much less lonely than he felt intensely. We know this not only because they went to great lengths to organize class dinners and picnics, but because they themselves created dining clubs in the fraternities in those years, fragmented and imperfect versions of the commons.

But what of the dorms themselves? They are convenient, surely, and they gather the students into groups near the library and the classrooms. Would a college be much worse off without them—with the students dispersed, as European students typically are, in *pensions* and apartments around the town and in the nearby countryside? There is a wonderful passage in the writer P. F. Kluge's memoir of a year teaching at Kenyon College, his alma mater, in which he calls the dormitory where he stayed for a semester "the anti-college":

> I'll never again make the mistake of thinking of dormitories as part of the college. They are the anti-college, college refuted, an opposing universe, negative and opposite, a building-beast where animals play golf hockey, swinging golf clubs, using the ball like a hockey puck, racketing at midnight right above my head, a place where animals nest in cages filled with comic books, video games, pizza boxes, unwashed clothing, and endless noise.[4]

Kluge found comfort, months later, in the thought that, bad as it was, his dormitory was a welcome relief after faculty meetings.

The dormitories at their best contribute to the endless seminar that I felt in the first few months of college and that you should feel. People will tell you, as my father told me, that you will learn more out of class than in class. "How do you mean?" I remember asking him. "You'll see," he said. "It's not all study. There will be bull sessions, you'll make friends talking late into the night, over meals." He said it with all the wistfulness of a Depression kid who had to put himself through night school and board with an aunt and uncle.

A student friend says that the good dorms are not the ones with the best rooms but those with the best hallways: one over the dining commons is his favorite; he wants a dorm with good "hallway culture"; "with something going on outside the doorway at any given moment of the day or night." A good dormitory is quiet enough for study yet, like a good city street, active with people and conversation until late at night. Like the college itself, the dormitories should bring students together from around the country and around the world, from backgrounds that differ and occasionally clash.

The reason I oppose fraternities so strongly is because they tend to close down this exchange and limit it to like minds from like backgrounds.

Let me be very specific: we sometimes preach to you that your roommates or your classmates, in their diversity of backgrounds, will teach you a great

---

4. P. F. Kluge, *Alma Mater: A College Homecoming* (Reading, Massachusetts, Addison-Wesley Publishing Co., 1993), pp. 70–71.

deal about the world. Is this true? Is *that* what I learned from them? I can't back up this wisdom with much from my own experience. Felix and I became friends. We talked endlessly. But at the end of an academic year together I knew only a little more about Gambia than I knew at the outset. (To be precise, I knew three additional facts: that Wolof was the predominant native language; that peanuts were the main crop; and that Bathurst, small as it was, had a flourishing taxi service belonging to his mother.) He knew one American much better, but did he know *America* better? I doubt it. What we both had learned was to like each other, to get around our differences, to break through to the things that we had in common.

What you also learned from your roommates is something very particular about yourself: how spoiled you can be, how fussy, how much effort it takes for you to get along at close quarters with someone who is simply different. And different not so much because they grew up thousands of miles away or in a different setting or with different resources—different because of the most elementary difference: they are not you; they do not react as you do or in harmony with you. Hegel said there is no individual. What he meant was that the self is a self only in relation to others. You will learn from your roommates and hallmates and classmates that it is hard to be neighbors, that it takes work. I hope you will learn as well that it is worth it.

Many college leaders over the years have emphasized the moral tasks of education. In the earliest years this was often a matter of religion. Colleges had a duty to see to the moral and religious formation of their students. By Coolidge's time, the pious ardors of faculty and president burned at a lower temperature. The duty of the college was more this-worldly and citizenly. "Character," said President Stearns of Amherst in 1872, "is of more consequence than intellect."[5] Courses, even required courses, could only accomplish so much with respect to the shaping of strong and virtuous characters.

---

5. Information about Calvin Coolidge at Amherst comes from the excellent book by Hendrik Booraem V, *The Provincial: Calvin Coolidge and His World, 1885–1895* (Lewisburg, Pa.: Bucknell University Press, 1994).

THE COLLEGE COMMUNITY

The residences, meals, the gymnasium, sports—all these answered to the sense that character was what was really at stake in the rigors of college.

As individuals, we must still put character before intellect; but as a college we must put intellect first. That is our competence and our institutional purpose. Neither our curriculum nor our residential and extracurricular life will guarantee you a good or strong character. Yet there is an ambiguity in our rejection of the old character-building and moral tutelage. Implicit in what we do are moral convictions and moral commitments of our own.

A good college has extraordinary human and material resources; it will present you with extraordinary opportunities. Every day you will have to choose among them: to take French or Arabic or Chinese; to push yourself into fields you don't know or to hang back safely; to try a new sport or the radio or the paper or start a magazine; to stick with friends on a Saturday night or at lunch or introduce yourself to someone new. Alumni press me wherever I go about core curriculums. Choice is the real core of any modern curriculum: informed, knowing, *free* choice.

Nor do we leave one another to make choices without challenge. Classes, laboratories, studios, and games—all these structure and discipline but also challenge your choices. The faculty will challenge your intellectual choices at every turn; so will your classmates.

The challenge of the residential system is more tacit: we have put it here in large part so that you can make the most of our curriculum: not only are your classes and laboratories and the library virtually at your door, but your lives are taken care of—meals served, entertainment provided, and friends and acquaintances gathered nearby. It creates a *free* way of life, free of many of the small duties that clutter life for most of the rest of us most of the time. If you do not quite "fish in the morning and edit in the afternoon," as Karl Marx once lyrically described an imaginary socialism, you do study Japanese in the morning, sociology or psychology at noon, argue politics over lunch, run the hills at dusk, and act in a play (or write one) in the evening.

All of this is artifice: a feat of human craft and design, for the college, like a plane or boat, is a structure that we have put together with great thought and at great expense. What does it *do*, really? What's it for? The simplest statement I can give is that it helps us to choose—intellectually, of course, but because intellect itself serves larger human ends, it helps us to choose the lives we will lead and the work we will do. In helping us to choose as knowingly and freely as possible, it helps us to make the most of our lives, to make them the best lives we can live, for ourselves and for others. This is a moral end, and we should embrace it without any postmodern diffidence or embarrassment.

Honesty, openness, a passion for the truth: these are plainly the ingredients we reward—and dishonesty and the like, if discovered, we scorn. In the classroom you will look to the faculty for guidance as you learn to make the well-informed intellectual choices that are the basis of a good intellectual life. In the dormitories there are no faculty. A college is not a boarding school, and faculty members do not intrude much into the residence lives of students.

To room with another person is to be forced to converse about the most basic order of the room and the day: you sleep here and I there; you put your stuff over here; what time shall we set the alarm for, and when shall we be quiet. It is to make oneself vulnerable to the other—in one's person, in one's goods, and, if there is any trust at all, in one's ideas and ideals. To share the campus with others is not so different. We are not always open to one another; we cannot always trust one another; we cannot always trust ourselves. A hundred identities can rear themselves up to separate us in anger or anxiety: athletes against aesthetes, men against women, poets against scientists, race against race, and so on.

I hope that tolerance is only the first lesson you learn by living and working together here. I hope that campus life pushes you further than that. I would like to say—I would like to hope—that it pushes us all toward the most difficult and elusive form of knowledge, and the one on which, morally, all the others depend: a knowledge of oneself.

Of Hatred and Bridges

Once you've been in college for a while, you know all too well the travails of scholarship: the all-nighter, the tremors of caffeine, the sense that footnotes are the inventions of evil professors and that grades—particularly on senior theses—are inherently unjust. Still, you may recall at least some joy in the enterprise. Among the joys of study, discovery is surely the greatest. You go along, reading, or talking, or brewing in the laboratory, and then, all of a sudden, you find something that you did not know was there—and that no one or next to no one knew. That it *was* there all along, covered up, forgotten, unnoticed, is a condition of discovery. "To discover," as Wallace Stevens put it well, "is not to invent." It is not a creation outside of you, but one within you, the creation of knowledge in its most palpable form.

The humblest of discoveries for most of us at college has been books. "Have you seen the new book on this?" "Have you read so-and-so; it's close to your topic." Professors, if they do nothing else, point the way (along the path of their own reading) to discoveries they have made and that you may make in your turn.

When I was a senior in college, steeped in the ancient Greeks and Hegel and Marx, an anthropology professor of mine, someone who had hoped that I would major in his subject, told me to read a book by one of the great anthropologists of his youth. The book, when I found it, was a small set of essays called *The Primitive World and its Transformations*, by Robert Redfield. To me, at least, it was a great discovery. It seemed to bring together my interest in moral philosophy with an interest in culture, as lived in small, often isolated villages. What fascinated Redfield above all was the tension between the accepted ways of any given culture, its own sense of right and wrong, and the more universal or cosmopolitan pull of certain ideals found everywhere in human beings.

One of the great stories of the book is of the young Pawnee chief Petalesharoo, and his rejection of the traditions of an annual human sacrifice to the Morning Star. Petalesharo's father had called on his fellow tribesmen to give up the practice; but this group of Loup Pawnee refused to stop, believing it would jeopardize the harvest. Then, around 1818, Petalesharoo stepped forward, with a young captive already bound to a post, and said that either he would die or she would go free. Stunned, if not necessarily convinced, his tribesmen stood back as he untied her, put her on his packhorse, and rode off with her to set her free among her own people.

Petalesharoo's deed is not one that we can ever fully fathom or describe: it comes to us in secondhand reports, from English-speaking scouts in the frontier territory, where he and his people were in retreat from an agonizing conquest. What stands out, nonetheless, is his courage: He rebels against an inherited tradition of hatred. He refuses to participate, or to allow others to continue, needless cruelty against ethnic enemies. He offers to die to save someone whom he may not have known and whom he had been taught to despise. In doing what he did—in acting on what must have been his own moral discovery of the uselessness of hatred—he exiled himself from a smaller world to a larger one, a larger one that had no certain place for him.

OF HATRED AND BRIDGES

This exile, this passage from the small world to the big, is, in a sense, the great human story of learning, from Adam and Eve on down. All of us go out, time and again, from the worlds of our mothers and fathers, from our families, from our schools, from our colleges and countries. What we go out *to* is a bigger world made up of smaller worlds, like our own, but worlds less and less sheltered from one another, more now than ever as travel and trade pull us all into one world economy and one world history. It is in and through discovery, through learning about other worlds and the limits of our own, that the story renews itself and draws us in.

As you go out from here, learning and discovering as you go, I worry that we have said too little about the one thing that Petalesharoo had to unlearn: hatred.

Despite the breadth of our curriculum, and the many courses that touch on prejudice and discrimination, we may not in the end have said enough to you about hating, the fierce emotion that eats up not only lives but nations, small worlds as well as large. You will leave us, in the small world, for a larger world in which hatred almost prevails. Sometimes I am not sure we have prepared you for it, much less prepared you to do something about it. It is easy for us humans to hate, it seems. It comes to us naturally: it comes over us in anger even toward those we love. Early on, we learn to say that we hate the one who has left us out in a game or wrecked the sand tower we made. Anyone who has reared a child has heard the tearful rebuke of frustration, "I hate you, Daddy; I hate you, Mommy."

Hatred as frustration—and, in particular, as the frustration of love—is a simple, powerful and engulfing emotion, one that we all know in ourselves and in others, even as little children. It causes us to hurt one another; from time to time it causes us to kill one another. It wells up in us as rage—and then, almost always, it subsides. Nowhere can we escape from it for long, and certainly not on a college campus. Of this form of hatred—the hot hatred of rage—you had plenty of experience long before you came to college; and you knew it here as well, in an incident in the dorm or an exchange on the field. But there is a deeper, more enduring strain in hatred that can hold it in place when emotions go cold. Call it cold hatred, the hatred that calculates and then acts.

When I was four or five, my two older brothers had a fight in the newly plowed dirt of the cornfield next to our house. I remember the bright sun of spring on the dark, soft earth in which you could not run because your shoes sank into the moist dirt. Pierce was nine or ten, I guess, and Peter a year and half younger. They must have been enraged at each other to be willing to go down onto the ground fighting. I have no recollection at all of how it began or what grudge or grievance was behind it. There was a hurried, awkward struggle, flailing arms and legs and torsos squared off against each other. Suddenly Pierce sat on Peter's chest, his arms stretched out to pin his younger brother's arms to the ground. Peter grumbled but wouldn't surrender. It seemed to me that he tried to keep a faint smile of defiance for his older brother. Pierce shouted, "Give up; give up." I and two or three younger kids watched in silence—and dread.

Then I quietly stepped up to where Peter's head lay on the ground and, saying nothing, twice kicked dirt at his mouth. Pierce told me to get away. Peter spat and blinked but otherwise barely acknowledged what I had done.

I ran away to the house and hid out somewhere upstairs.

I'm not sure that I hated Peter at all when I kicked the dirt at him: I was by no means caught up in the hot surge of emotion that had so suddenly overtaken him and Pierce. In fact, as I recall it now, I and the other little children there with me were terrified as much of the rage we saw as of the actual shoves and punches exchanged by my two older brothers. Yet seeing Peter down, and momentarily powerless, I saw a chance to get back at him and a chance, for a time, to get away with it.

The desire for vengeance is understandable: Peter and I didn't fight *all* the time; he had better things to do with his time than feud with a kid four years younger. But when we fought—when I challenged him—he responded with brutal efficiency by folding his middle finger into a small tight triangle and jabbing it hard into my solar plexus, leaving me writhing on the ground unable, for a few seconds, to breathe.

What interests me now in this episode out of memory is not the passion of it, for there was almost none. It is the peculiarly truncated rationality I felt: "I will get back at him, *now;* I will avenge myself."

I must have known that it could not possibly end there and that I was doing myself no lasting good. For Pierce, Peter, and the younger children there, what I had done was a breach of every backyard canon of honor and fair fighting. Peter would catch up with me sooner or later, exacting a retribution at least as grievous as the injuries that made me yearn for vengeance.

But for now he was powerless; Pierce was busy keeping him down; for a few moments no one could check my own desire to hurt and humiliate him. Our brief history as brothers had taught me his power and his own coolly rational methods with me; he hit me when he pleased and more or less as he pleased. The punch to the solar plexus was simply the most effective technique for him, leaving me powerless to retaliate, as ever, but also powerless to tattle or even scream. So I wanted my revenge; here was my chance; "take it and run," I said to myself.

I had other playground fights as a kid. I resented a teacher or two. And I've exchanged angry words with colleagues or strangers. (Once, at sixteen, after football practice, I took a swing at someone who would grow up to be a colleague, although, I am authorized to say, not a present colleague.) But I cannot say that I have known much of the systematic and almost irrepressible hatred—what I will call the cold hatred—that daily works itself out here in America and around the world.

Real hatred, cold hatred, requires, first of all, an idea. "I will avenge myself," I said in my own cold decision to kick dirt in Peter's face. I wanted to humiliate him. In ideologies of hatred the idea approaches the ruling force of an ideal because, in its hold on the will and imagination, it seems to drive away all other ideas—of restraint, of fairness, of the consequences for ourselves and, above all, for others of what we do and talk of doing.

In Ireland once, my wife and I gave a ride to a little boy—stout and dark-haired with a square, even face. "And what would you like to do when you grow up?" I asked. "I'd like to go up north to join the Provos," he told me.

"And what would you do for them?" "Throw bombs and shoot the British," he said, with the earnest expression of any child picking out an admired profession to which he aspires.

Real hatred lasts in ways that love, by contrast, rarely can. It seems a much easier legacy to pass on to the young and the innocent. We have, most of us, as Swift once said, enough religion to hate, but not enough to love.

Real hatred seems to grow when the conditions favor it.

Powerlessness, even momentary powerlessness, abets hatred and allows it to flourish. The great insight of constitutions is that no power should go without its check, and that unbalanced powers will allow passions, including hatred, to rule us in such a way as to destroy us. We believe in checks and balances because we believe that no one in power can be trusted unchecked and without counterbalance. Given the power, each of us is capable, at the right time and under the right circumstances, of great evil.

Ignorance seems as necessary for systematic, calculating hatred as oxygen is to fire. Moral ignorance bars us from fathoming the suffering of others, because we have reduced them—if only for a moment—to something less, and less important, than ourselves. Simone Weil, the French mystic, defined violence as whatever transforms human beings into things. Zygmunt Bauman, in his writings on the Holocaust, suggests that modern societies and bureaucracies may have a peculiar aptitude for distancing, for placing other human beings within the reach of our actions and decisions but outside the sphere of our sympathy and understanding.

Finally, fear feeds hatred: a fear nurtured in ignorance and aggravated by all the stray, hostile emotions that plague us as a species. "You are different—in your customs, appearance, values; you have something that I want; you cannot be trusted with my family, my school or neighborhood, my land, my life." Nature has taught us to fear our differences; we must learn, sometimes against odds, to trust and value them.

In the years that you spend at college, you will find new names for hatred as you see it triumph or flare near and far: sometimes it is as brief as the shouted or graffitied insult; sometimes it is as dangerous and destructive as a bombing; in Rwanda it built and built as a conviction until people who

OF HATRED AND BRIDGES

were neighbors or even cousins turned on one another in murder. I will evoke here only one of the names we now link to the ravages of a systematic and calculating hatred; that name is Bosnia.

We tend to make a romance of the land itself, because of its beauty, because of its suffering, and perhaps because, as Americans, we cherish what it seems to have once represented and now has lost, probably forever: its tolerance of differences.

It is an important point of history to say that this romance, like most others, rests on a kind of distortion, a putting aside or forgetting of more uncomfortable realities. Ivo Andric, the great novelist of Bosnia, has a diplomat comment on what he calls "this cramped, hilly, starveling patch of ground":

> There are four religions living [here]. Each of them is exclusive and keeps strictly apart from the others. . . . And each of them considers that its own welfare and advantage are dependent on the ruin and decline of the other three religions and that the other three can only advance at its expense. And each of them has made intolerance the highest virtue. . . .

The great image in Andric's work is that of the bridge, large or small, of wood or stone or iron. Bridges held his country together through winters, wars, the collapse of empires, and the rise of new tyrannies. Bridges and roads united people whose remoteness was sometimes the only guarantee of tolerance.

In a beautiful prose poem about bridges, Andric enumerates the many kinds he admired during his long life in Bosnia: "Great stone bridges . . . their sharply chiseled lines worn down. . . . Slender iron bridges, stretched from one shore to the other like a wire, shaking and resounding with every train that hurtles over them. . . . Wooden bridges on the way into the little town . . . whose furrowed planks sink and creak under the hooves of the village horses. . . ." He particularly recalls the most impermanent and simple ones, "those tiny bridges in the mountains, nothing but a largish tree trunk or two logs riveted together, thrown across a wild stream that would be impassable without them." Sometimes twice in a year they are washed out, but the people then cut and lay down new ones.

All bridges, he says, are "equally worthy of our attention, for they point out places where a man came across an obstacle and did not turn away, but overcame it and bridged it as best he could...." Hatred, like the streams of Bosnia, can be bridged; and even where the bridges themselves go down—or are pulled down, like the beautiful stone bridge of Mostar—they can be rebuilt.

A college is in its way a bridge. You gather in your first year, from different places and with different notions, and we say to you little more than this: talk to one another, study alongside one another, meet on the bridges that are courses, books, plays, laboratories. And you, like Andric's Bosnians, responded in many ways, not always perhaps the best ways—occasionally even in ways that may be harmful to one another. But on the whole you get along; the bridge holds.

In the midst of national and international doubt about the value of inclusion—of integration—the college is a kind of Sarajevo: a place where the differences among us have themselves made up a kind of curriculum, a course of study, a path of discovery. An Amherst College policy once explained our commitment to inclusion in these words: "We do [this] for the simplest, but most urgent, of reasons: because the best and the brightest people are found in many places, not few; because our classrooms and residence halls are places of dialogue, not monologue; because teaching and learning at their best are conversations with persons other than ourselves about ideas other than our own."*

Whatever the fate of Bosnia, of the many Bosnias in which tolerance must vanquish hate, remember the small wooden bridges that Andric praised. Let them be metaphors for your work and your life. Bridge the waters that rush down our human hills and threaten to cut us off from one another. Bridge hatred, in particular, and never despair if it washes out one bridge; build it again the way his Bosnians did. Build better, if you can, but above all build again.

---

*May 25, 1996. Affirmative Action Policy Statement of the Board of Trustees of Amherst College.

Pilgrims, Scholars, and Hitchhikers

When I was a little younger than the freshmen gathered here today, I went on a pilgrimage. It was a religious pilgrimage, to the cathedral at Chartres, and drew students from all over Europe and beyond. It was only a two- or three-day affair, but we hiked several thousand strong along back lanes, among great golden fields in the farm country outside Paris. We camped out, we sang, we argued about religion and how we ought to live our lives. On the last night, we marched uphill into the village with candles in our hands. The steep streets filled with faint ambling lights. It seemed for a moment like the fourteenth century. I had never done anything like this before. Except for marches on Washington and New York in the '60s and '70s, I have never done anything like it since. I recall it today because of the powerful sense it gave me of belonging to a faith, to a march, to a purpose. Long after I had abandoned the faith (and I was none too sure of it at the time), I remembered the bonfire, the arguments, the sense of oneness with this small army of religiously earnest European university students.

I want to talk about the sense of community and its place in your experience—in our experience. In taking up this theme, I know that it is at once an elusive and sensitive one, taken up many times before by deans and presidents, here and elsewhere. A couple of generations ago no one talked about community because everyone took it for granted. Places like this were made up then of young men from pretty similar backgrounds, some richer and some poorer, a few from overseas and a few on scholarship. Was the sense of community stronger then than now? At the very least, it was easier to assume, if not to achieve.

I speak of a *sense* of community, not simply community. I have several reasons for this: First, the community of a college is not something I can talk about now with much confidence or certainty. Like the new students, I have just arrived and look around with eyes that may or may not conceal bewilderment and anticipation. Second, I would hope, by speaking of my sense of community, to pull this concept a little closer to my own experience. We can be fairly sure, most of the time, of our own feelings about an ideal, even an indeterminate one. Finally, I want to begin and end this talk with a slight distance or detachment from the ideal of community. And I say this not out of cynicism or even skepticism about the ideal we invoke with the word community.

I believe in community, but I believe in it more or less the way I believe in love. We seek it more often than we find it; we find it in odd and surprising ways; it is real but it is also fragile, uncertain, and sometimes ambiguous.

In a wonderful if pompous image, Hegel once said that the owl of Minerva—the classical symbol of wisdom—spreads her wings in flight only when night falls. We can never understand an age, he suggests, until it is gone, or going. Community may be an ideal that grows more vivid the more we are estranged from its reality—in neighborhoods, countries, or colleges.

Let me begin with the help of an earlier president. Coming out of the faculty, where he taught and wrote about American history and culture, John

PILGRIMS, SCHOLARS, AND HITCHHIKERS

William Ward engaged in a bold act of protest early on in his Amherst College presidency. In the spring of 1972, he made a small pilgrimage of his own to the Westover Air Force Base. There he led a protest and was arrested along with many professors and students. This brave but controversial act put him at the center of a bitter divide about where the expression of personal conviction ended and the responsibilities of his office started.

He gave a poignant convocation talk on community in the college chapel a few years later, in 1976. What he said then is striking to me in its directness and honesty about the college community. I have to believe that what happened at Westover shaped his reflections.

The scholarly roots of our use of the word *community* seemed clear to President Ward: as the discipline of sociology invented itself out of history and philosophy in the latter part of the nineteenth century, some of its greatest figures, in England, France, and Germany, distinguished among historical periods by creating typologies of various ways of living. Like the philosophers who inspired them, they saw one model emerging from another. Often the typologies were set at poles to one another, status versus contract, sentiment versus rationality, and so on.

The important typology for Bill Ward was the one that every student in sociology and political science learns in German, the typology of *Gesellschaft* and *Gemeinschaft*. There is a kind of hot and cold in this dichotomy, a yin and yang. We usually translate *Gesellschaft* as *society*: it represents rationality, contract, and purpose in human relations, often without regard to feeling. In everyday German, *eine Gesellschaft* can be a company, a corporation, or a large gathering. *Gemeinschaft*, on the other hand, means community, and represents warmth and intimacy, with roles or status assigned not by contract but by givens like birth and kinship. Ward stated with no hesitation that Amherst represented the former rather than the latter: as we consider a college, he said, clearly we are an instance of *Gesellschaft*, a contractual association. We come together from fifty states and foreign countries by virtue of what we can do, not by reason of who we are. We are not kin, we did not grow together in the same neighborhood, we are not bound by a common faith or an ethnic identity. It may sound cold to put it this way, he suggested, but it is the truth.

At this distance from his speech it is easy to say both how right he was about this, and how wrong. We are a contractual, rational association, bound together by our purposes, but we are also one that is small, residential and suffused with ideals about mutual concern, support, and friendship.

The typology of *Gemeinschaft* and *Gesellschaft* pushes us, I think, toward exaggerated exclusions, toward either/or's: it is this or that, rational or irrational, contracted or else assumed. But communities, as I have known them, are something of both. Yes, purposes structure communities and bind them under duress. Still, communities remain compounds of purpose and feeling, thought and emotion, ideals and histories.

"We come together," Bill Ward said, "not out of love or friendship but for learning." Yet it is precisely this purpose, our shared commitment to learning, that can make us friends and allies in our enterprise.

In an archaic usage we should never abandon, professors and students are both scholars: we are schooling together, inquiring together, the students hitching rides, as it were, and the professors offering them. That is the heart of any curriculum. Bill Ward himself spoke more than once of "the fellowship of the mind." His words are not so very far from those of Janet Morgan in the late Henry Mishkin's "Hymn to Amherst": "Those who teach and those who learn," she said, "build a living city"—a living community. In another verse, she spoke of the college as "bound by friendship's charter."

Yet communities of learning can and must have an edge to them. Armour Craig, a professor and once acting president of Amherst College, liked to say that a college faculty is characterized by a certain irritability of mind. I take it that he meant the phrase in an almost wholly physiological sense: not that we are a grumpy, irritable lot, but rather that the faculty is sensitive, at times acutely sensitive, to the world around it, to changes, nuances, differences: in short, to ideas. Craig's metaphor touches on a core notion of intelligence as liveliness of mind and thought. It also suggests the necessary irritation that characterizes teaching and learning. In one of Plato's dialogues,

Socrates styled himself a rayfish, with a sting sharp enough to stir his pupils to learning.

Most of us have experienced a sense of community in other settings: on teams perhaps; with the stage crew and actors in a play; in a synagogue or church; when relatives gather for a family wedding. Sometimes that sense of community is keen, though fleeting. I remember this feeling as a hitchhiker with Adelia, in the years before we were married (when hitchhiking felt safe). Someone would pick us up, at an empty intersection on the edge of Wichita, say, someone who might be scruffy or neat, drunk or sober. There was joy in their stopping for us, often after a long wait or a sweaty trudge out of town. (In Vermont, I remember, you could hitchhike for half a day with no one stopping at all, as if the thumb up on an outreached arm was understood there as a sign of malevolence, or perhaps quarantine.)

Whenever someone did stop, there was always a variant of the same question: How far are you going? Where are you headed? On these questions hung a lot, for both sides. Do I tell them exactly where I am going? How much can I trust them with this information? Maybe they are up to no good.

Once, outside of Denver, a man in a Mustang picked us up at dusk. He said he was headed for Illinois—more than a thousand miles away. After a while, he asked if I drove. Sure; we both do, I said. Well then how about one of you take the wheel while I sleep? We drove all night, as he slept in the back, at a speed you could do even then only in the West. He let us off at dawn the next day on an interchange outside Chicago.

I offer this example because it is dear to me, and because it gives us the barest elements of any community: we were all headed in the same direction; we were all in a hurry; he was sleepy but had a fast car; Adelia and I were wide awake with the excitement of our trip; both of us could drive. The three of us had a common purpose and matching needs and strengths. It was a contract all right, but there was warmth in it, a sense of openness to one another, to a brief, purposeful friendship, requiring a brief but palpable trust. Not least, in the foggy dawn outside Chicago, there was gratitude.

When one freely chosen way crosses another, when one person can help another on the way, there is an exhilaration, a delight in a kind of friendship, if only for a limited purpose, if only for a time.

You can learn a lot on your own, I know. But think for a moment of how much of what we learn we learn from others. Every kind of instrument with which we learn was invented by someone and painstakingly perfected by others. The car, the shoe, the course, the college: all of these are the handiwork of people like us, setting out on paths and trying to figure out ways to make them smoother. None of us can deny the ambiguities of human invention and learning. The power of knowing is a power for good and evil. But it is a power multiplied many times over because we human beings are teachers to one another. We learn from what others have learned before us.

A college like this one has three essential features of human architecture: First, and most important, it is built around a specific relation between teachers and students, a relation that I call, simply, teaching as conversation. Second, it is built around a relation between its scholars—all of them—and their scholarship, a relation of commitment, often passionate commitment, to the ongoing refinement of the intellectual disciplines in which we acquire and organize knowledge. And third, it is built in the faith that students will learn much of what they can learn from one another, in conversations in the dormitory and dining hall; in arguments on the playing fields and in the laboratories; in discussions in theaters, studios, and coffeehouses. All of these conversations will fail utterly if we have too little confidence in one another, too little trust, to engage each other passionately and seriously.

The nub of what I want to say is this: the college community is an instrument of learning and exploration. Never let it become morally small or imaginatively confining. The differences among you will serve your learning. The obvious differences are those of background—of race, of gender, of outlook, and origin. But the less obvious differences will serve you even more, the differences of intellectual temperament and approach, of insights that compete, of conclusions that clash. Across all of these differences there will be, I am sure, friendship and warmth and gratitude. But there will also be anger, disappointment in one another, and what we call too lightly disillusion.

Do I sound too much like Walt Whitman if I say: all of this is to the good, to the purpose?

The community we have at a college—the community we seek at a college—is not one of unalloyed warmth and fellowship and commonality. Neither rigor nor freedom in our learning will flourish without sharpness and passion and difference. Conflict and argument are essential to you and essential to what we do here. Do not shy from conflict in your learning any more than you shy from complexity. Respect one another, but challenge one another. Get to the bottom of your—our—conflicts. What are the principles we argue over? Which are the prejudices? Fight hard where you feel you must. But never presume that you are completely right and your colleagues completely wrong. Understand what separates you as well as what joins you.

There was a time, and it was a long time, when colleges were all of one race, one gender, one region of one country. That time is gone. The community of that time was no doubt a good one, where learning and teaching held challenges and glories of their own. But the community of our time can be immeasurably better. We know all too well what stands in our way. We are diverse in more ways than we can count. We live in an age of suspicion and mistrust. There may be much to fear from our world, and from one another. But the very multiplicity of our selves makes community a more thrilling and more rigorous achievement for all of us. From out of our differences, we can learn—and we can teach. And the community we create here, on this hill, will stand as a model for the communities we must build together throughout this land and throughout our world.

Of Sex and Self

Presidents at colleges big and small are generally kept around for obscure purposes. Whatever these purposes are, they seem to require daily attendance at lots of meetings in a dark business suit. You can't miss the president at these meetings: everybody else seems to be dressed much more comfortably and having a much better time. Gray hair is helpful; but if you don't have it when you arrive, it will sprout soon enough. For the most part, presidents are nicely treated; they put them in a white house at the entrance to the college with lots of big windows so you can catch sight of them during their off hours—like lions at the zoo. They sign lots of papers and shake lots of hands. In crises they are expected to do something, or at least to say something. And twice a year, as school begins and as school ends, they are supposed to say something significant. Being new to this presidential task, I'm not sure just what to say. My only guide in this is my own sense of what is important—to the faculty, the staff, but most of all, what is important to you, the students.

THE COLLEGE COMMUNITY

I want to say something about a different division in our lives, in this case an inescapable division, one given to us in our biology. That division is one which, like race, can either bring us together to enrich our lives or pull us apart to make our lives harsher and more painful.

That division, of course, is sex. It is perhaps especially important to you, as undergraduates, at the moment when you move out from your families into your own lives as adults, gradually establishing a sense of confidence in your identity, in your personal style, in *your* ways of relating to all people, but especially to your intimates and friends of both sexes. Your interpretation of your own gender is likely to develop and crystallize in the next four years. You will seek to forge an adult identity strong enough—steely enough—to survive the rigors of human adventure. None of you, however privileged, can expect an easy life: for human beings there is no such thing.

Sexuality is an important part of your life. It marks the biological division within our species and virtually all others. We find differentiated sex roles and gender expectations again and again in human culture and society. Often these roles and expectations frustrate the aspirations of both women and men.

In the '60s and '70s lots of colleges admitted their first women undergraduates. I'm told it was an awkward, sometimes painful, beginning: a handful of young women came by invitation into the very traditional world of the all-male liberal arts college. Last year in the spring, we gathered—students, faculty, alumnae, and others—to talk over that awkward beginning, the twists and turns of coeducation in the years since, and our hopes for the future. We celebrated our triumphs, mulled over our defeats, and began to chart where we might go from here.

It was the ideal of twenty years ago, and of today, that men and women would integrate fully at this college. Men and women would come together as equals, in conversation, in politics and governance, in sport, but above all in intellect and aspiration. This ideal of equality across the sexes is as old as Plato's *Republic*. I am sure that no one thought it would be easy to achieve. I am also sure that no one foresaw just *how* hard it would be.

OF SEX AND SELF

Identity is always easiest the way Henry David Thoreau sought it, in solitude, in the quiet of the woods. All of us need to escape to our own Walden Pond at times, to breathe easy, to take notice of a world not shaped by human conventions, to listen for that different drummer Thoreau spoke of. Still, it was Thoreau who said, "It takes two to speak the truth . . . one to speak and another to hear." In a family, in a community, in a college, what you say and think even of yourself may not be heeded. In a community, your sense of identity—and equality—can be elusive. Some, as the pig said in George Orwell's *Animal Farm,* always end up being more equal than others.

Sex, like race, is a division whose social history tells a sober tale of the elusiveness of genuine equality. To those who say we have come a long way, we say, that is true, but we have a longer way still to go. A recent, quite telling study suggests that as women enter the work force, in search of equal pay and equal respect, they more often than not find themselves holding down a "second shift" of disproportionate household and family responsibilities that men somehow escape.

So, too, at college, despite our ideals, you may notice some subtle or not so subtle disproportions persisting between men and women. The fans are still more numerous at football than field hockey. Sometimes the press seems to pay more attention to men's events than to women's. Someone, whether male or female, may listen more intently to the males in campus discussion. Men may dominate a club or activity for no very good reason. The louder music and the bigger crowds are drawn to the weekend parties given by the remaining all-male fraternities.

The women who first enrolled in all-male colleges came with an adventurous spirit. They had the courage to be the first, to face resistance, resentment, and discrimination. They sought to change the campus—to develop new, equal, and shared traditions of schooling men and women. But they also wanted to prove something about equality and themselves: mixed in, even unequally, with men, they knew they could do *just fine,* thank you. And they did.

But here on campus, as in America, no liberation is fully accomplished until it is realized inwardly and personally as a part of our consciousness, a portion of our selves. What has confused us all along is the answer to the question: what are we *given* by our sexes? Our bodies are given to us in and through sex—we are female or we are male. And it does not in any way slight the importance of that gift to say that you have to decide what to do with it. You will shape it; you will define it. At a liberal arts college it is our faith that biology alone can never be destiny. Yes, you have a body that is female or male. But all the rest—the expectations, the roles, the subtle yeses and noes, "throwing like a girl" or "boys don't cry"—all of that isn't given at all. It's taken, it's chosen. The only question is: will you make your own choices, or let others impose them on you?

So long as we have time, so long as we have thoughts, we will have choices—choices about our bodies, but above all about our selves. The liberal arts curriculum, whatever else it is, studies those choices from as many different perspectives as we can encompass.

Our ideal of education is that *you* will choose, in gender and in all the other aspects of your life. You will choose, knowing that *much* is given in life—a time, a place, a body, a family, a nationality—but much, much else in life is to be chosen by you. These years of college, these untrammeled years, give you the freedom to reflect on your choices as you make them. Sometimes, like the existentialists Jean-Paul Sartre and Simone de Beauvoir, we can see choice as a leap of the mind. Life offers up its several possibilities. We look them over and select one. Choice *can* be like that, but not often.

Choice in relation to sex will rarely be so simple and definite. Maya Angelou says at the end of her memoir of childhood that "you don't have to think about doing the right thing. . . . If you're for the right thing, then you do it without thinking." Here's what I think she means: no matter how thoughtful you are, no matter how much you read and think and discuss, no matter how conscientious you are—choice as it builds toward identity and character, towards *who* you are—choice like that will sneak up on you in a thousand small incidents of action and reaction. Do you let someone silence you in an argument? Do you let a roommate tell you in words or gestures not to define yourself in some way because it's too effeminate or too mannish? Can someone, a little older, a little more confident, a little pushier, make you drink more than you want to, or engage in a personal relationship you don't want? Can that person at the extreme even draw you into a sexual relationship when you know deep down it's not what you want? Can others make you feel inadequate because you don't meet *their* expectations of your gender and identity?

Or looking at these questions another way, would you ever push another person to do or be something he has not chosen? Would you force her to go your way rather than hers—in drinking, in sexual conduct, in being? Never fail to hear another person's "no."

To be free in relation to sex is, above all, to think freely. And just as all writing, as Judge Cardozo had it, is *re*writing, so all thinking must be *re*thinking. You have to rethink yourself over and again. You have to be *for* that self even if others sometimes try to shame you out of it. And you have to choose that self in sustained and repeated acts over your whole life, acts of courage and acts of faith.

"Ain't I a woman?" asked Sojourner Truth, rhetorically. Her point was that she didn't need to be a man to walk all day or preach all night or lift great weights. "I can do all this," she says to us across a century, "I can do it *as a* woman." She might also say that you don't have to be a woman to nurture children or to display your deepest emotions honestly. All of that is humanly open to each of us, if only we are free enough to choose for ourselves.

You alone will have to rethink for yourself the great questions of sex and self, of friendship and intimacy, of work and family. The studies you undertake here should help you understand your choices. And understanding them, you will see why you can never, ever, let others make those choices for you.

STUDIES

In Praise of Rigor

Those of us who end up with these odd jobs, as college presidents, become perforce apologists—defenders and explainers—of what we are all about in liberal arts colleges.

Our teaching needs no defense, I suppose, since passing knowledge on from one person who knows a little more to another who knows a little less is so primitive, so basic, *so defining* an activity that we could almost say that to be human is to teach. We are a teaching species. (Research, too, conceived of as a disciplined exercise of curiosity, needs no more defense than to say that curiosity is among the most basic of human urges—and is at its best when carried out with discipline.)

In college, it is the *liberal* arts and sciences that are always in question. Which ones are *they*—and why teach *them*? Why do research in them? The simplest answer is freedom: they are the *liberating* arts—the studies that set us free.

But now comes the rub. Surely all study is liberating—from ignorance—

to knowledge, from servitude—to mastery. Why are *these* arts and sciences better than others? Why are history and math and dance better *liberators* than marketing and communications and accounting?

There are a hundred quicksilver adjectives that answer this—these arts are deeper, broader, more challenging, more satisfying, more fundamental. But I want to offer an even simpler answer. It is this: the liberal arts are better arts simply because they are harder, they are tougher; they require more discipline—and they reward it.

They are more rigorous.

Rigor is a word I put with *ambivalence* as an ideal. It's a word you see too often in tenure recommendations. And yes, Rocky Mountain toughness, as William James called it, is a favored intellectual stance. But there's also *rigor mortis*—the stiffness of death; there's inflexibility, and the rigor of resistance to ideas. There's the movement in church circles called *rigorism*—an excess of requirements and severity in moral life. . . . I am reminded of Wittgenstein's imaginary game consisting only of rules—where play becomes impossible.

So why rigor? For all its negatives, rigor has a specific meaning that suits us well in the liberal arts.

Rigor suggests: First, *exactness* in terms and measures and standards. *This is not that.* Second, rigor suggests the *will* to make exactness stick, to carry it out, to impose it on oneself and others. (Orwell was thrilled at the thought that in building an airplane a certain part works best at so many centimeters and not one more. All of us have had the sense in reading a poem that it is perfect just as it is; nothing can be added or subtracted without ruining it.

Aristotle in the *Nicomachean Ethics* speaks of *akríbeia*—precision or exactitude. The passage in which this comes up is a wonderful one in Book I, Chapter 3. (Aristotle is talking about the craft of politics or political things.) My own translation goes like this: "We will have adequately explained these things," he says, "if we can make them as clear as their nature permits. Precision—*akríbeia*—is not the same in all the inquiries we pursue, no more than it is in all the crafts. The beautiful and the just, these are what we are trying to learn about in this political art. But many differences of opinion and errors occur in this field, so that it seems sometimes to be solely a matter of opinion with no objectivity.

"We should be pleased in discussing these things," he goes on, "if we can give even a rough sketch of the truth. An educated person seeks *that precision or exactness* in *each class* of things which the nature of the thing permits—it seems as silly to expect mathematicians to give merely persuasive arguments as to expect lawyers or rhetoricians to give mathematical proofs." In other words, don't try to be any more exact—any more rigorous—than the field of study allows.

Aristotle states an ideal of exactness tempered by a sense of the inexactness of the world itself.

We know all too well that we can be exact about some very trivial things: how many times the second Justice Harlan used the words "tradition" or "traditional" in his Supreme Court opinions is less important than how he insisted on the uses of tradition in constitutional law.

Throughout the *Nicomachean Ethics* Aristotle speaks of the importance of what he calls *skopos*—we translate it as *aim*. But it is a word not entirely lost to us in our own talk of the *scope* of study or inquiry.

To make our disciplines liberating to ourselves and to our students, we need rigor in the way we go about our inquiries, but we also need rigor in the inquiries we pursue. *The aim, the scope of inquiry, must itself be rigorous.*

My favorite Greek sentence comes from Socrates in the *Apology*. "The unexamined—or unchallenged—life is not worth living."

The rigorous questions appropriate to the liberal arts are questions that challenge or examine all that we do, and all that we are, and all that we believe in; they are questions that challenge the way we live—and what we live for.

They are big questions but also small. What's the nature of justice? But also, what is the nature of hydroxylation of amino acids? The rigor in these questions, the hardness in them, comes of both the discipline, the precision, with which we try to answer them, but also the *scope*—the aim—that we have in mind as we set about our processes of inquiry.

A colleague of mine in constitutional law once told me that on certain questions it is hard to get the students in your sights. He is a hunter and imagined his students at exam time in the sights of his intellectual rifle. Sometimes, in some fields, one answer argues out about as well as another. Certainly in law we know that to be so. There is rigor in argument, as Aristotle suggested, without it necessarily leading to one right answer.

The twofold rigor of the liberal arts, then, is this: we must be rigorous in our procedures—our arguments, our computations, our experiments—but also in our use of those procedures to ask truly rigorous, challenging questions of ourselves and of our students.

Sometimes it will seem to us—and certainly to the parents of our students—that these arts are useless. They bake no bread and mend no fences. Their usefulness is much more general, much more enduring, and in its aim, much more rigorous, than the more obviously useful arts. For the rigors of living a free life involve much bigger questions, much harder questions, than how to make a living.

So when a student (or parent) asks *"Why* the liberal arts?" at least one fair answer is the simple one: they are more rigorous in the fullest and best sense. They are harder, intellectually, and make us better intellectuals—better scientists, poets, scholars, or businessmen.

Rigor states for us an ideal of challenging ourselves fully. But why should *that* ideal have moral status? Challenge is intellectually important: it pushes us, it extends us. It is physically important for the same reasons. It strengthens us. But why morally? How does it make us better to one another—or, for that matter, to ourselves?

Here again Aristotle is of real help. Happiness was one of the great moral themes of Greek philosophy. It's a theme we don't talk about much in this century. Joyce once said that only the fools are happy. Aristotle would have found that a bizarre statement, a statement in which happiness is absurdly reduced to simple contentment. To Aristotle happiness was a vigorous activity, not a state of rest. It was an energy, a working use of the soul. And happiness comes with those activities of the soul—the self—in which mastery and excellence are achieved.

Aristotle's vision, then, was of human fulfillment in the challenge, the discipline, of activities that made the most of our capacities—including the capacity to be good. It is still the most balanced vision I know, of life as we humans try to live it. Rigor is not merely an academic ideal, then, it is also a moral ideal.

My own sense is that while there are excesses galore in rigor—Captain Lynch of Galway hung his son and gave us lynchings in the name of rigorous justice, after all—rigor is still an *indispensable* moral ideal. Courage, Plato says somewhere, is the most fundamental of the virtues because all the rest depend on it. Courage is a kind of rigor—a toughness in the face of the most severe challenges. Rigor as a moral ideal says that we cannot make it through life happily, decently, unless we master dismaying challenges, frightful challenges, and survive not only challenge but tragedy. No amount of kindness or sympathy or fairness will help when a friend deserts us for lack of courage, for lack of rigor.

We need rigor in our moral lives just as much as in our intellectual. It gives the frame, the sturdiness, of courage to all the gentler virtues we treasure.

And so I say to our students, with Aristotle, seek rigor in all that you do; not an excess of rigor, certainly, but that amount of rigor that frees you to live your lives at their best—and happiest.

The Short Course

Before you get to college, you will spend days going through the course catalogue with a mixture of enthusiasm and dread utterly incomprehensible to outsiders. You can alternate, I am sure, between an impulse to take everything and an occasional urge to take nothing at all. You will wonder what intellectual and human virtues lie hidden in the names of obscure faculty. You can read the brief course descriptions the way some people pore over holiday brochures. You may even have the craven thought that it would be easier if they *told* you what to take. It's hard enough to choose a freshman seminar, never mind a year's worth of courses.

This is the liberal arts curriculum. I welcome you to its delights and desperations. Reduced to requirements, it can usually be summarized quickly: you must take four or five courses each semester for four years; you must take a first-year seminar in the fall; depending on the college, you may have to take one or two courses in science, fine arts, English; and within two years, you must choose at least one departmental or interdepartmental major with various requirements that you must complete in time for graduation.

Each year, when the Dean of Students and I stop in for conversation in the dormitories, the discussion goes back and forth over these matters. There is lots of talk about getting one's thirteenth choice in the first-year seminars or, more seriously, the large size of many of the courses that students choose in the first year. There is one constant in all this. When I ask how important curriculum was in the choice of a college, nearly everyone every time says that freedom of choice is what students want. There is no mystery about what students mean by the word *curriculum*, either. It means to them—to you— what the college requires of you, what courses you have to take to make it through to graduation.

I want to talk to you about your curriculum, but I want to do it in the larger context of college curricula, plural. More precisely, I want to tell you something about the many curricula that one college, Amherst, put forth over the century and three-quarters of its institutional life on this hill. I want to do this because I believe that curriculums will succeed or fail largely on the basis of your own choices and the knowledge and imagination that you bring to these choices. It can be the best curriculum for you; it can also be, if not the worst, still a sharp disappointment.

Let me begin with the word itself. *Curriculum* is Latin for a little course, a short running course in track and field events. Early on, it became a metaphor for the run of life or work. *Career* is another such word, also from Latin and its descendants, and also embodying a kind of dead metaphor about life as a race. The words *curriculum vitae*—course of life—sum this up almost too neatly. So let me be clear at the outset: our curriculum is not a race; many good students who make it through do so with a year or two off. What is helpful in the etymology is the sense of the whole, and perhaps the idea that the whole is bigger—and certainly longer—than the parts that make it up.

A curriculum is often narrowly understood as a collection of courses, some required, some not. Its first usage in English was in seventeenth-century Scotland, where the Scottish universities described their courses of study with what many took to be a Latin diminutive: the curriculum was the "short" course, the brief description of the overall course of study, put in a few words and over some set term of years, three or four or five depending on the field. This is very close to present usage here and in many other places. I ask you all to keep this in mind as you begin your course of study. We can agree that it takes four years and thirty-two completed courses to earn a degree. But more important than the requirements is the sense that there is a course in this, a path through choices and requirements, one that you will be able to describe in various ways, now and as you go along and as you finish and look back on it. There should be surprises along the way, oddities, whimsy, serendipity; but there should also be themes and connections and some direction. Each of you should think of yourselves as having your own curriculum here, your own path and your own no doubt shifting ways of describing it.

When Amherst began, everything was required. Our students took what was offered and they took all of it, like everyone else in colleges in America in the early nineteenth century. They had no choices, nothing to elect within the curriculum. There were no majors. The course took four years and set you to learn Latin and Greek, some mathematics, a little general science, and lots of what we would now call theology. The president taught every senior in a course on morality. (Seniors probably still need presidential advice and direction, I acknowledge.) The fixed curriculum was offered in a more or less fixed spirit: these were truths that were taught, not opinions or interpretations. None of this was offered in the spirit of choice. And if human life, however regulated, remains always full of choice, the range of careers chosen by Amherst men in those days shows what now seems like remarkable unanimity. In keeping with Amherst's mission to educate poor young men for the worldwide ministry, nearly all of them went on to be Congregational ministers and teachers of religion—often in mission outposts where they founded colleges and schools after the Amherst model.

Amherst was founded with a point of view, and bad grades and suspension would come to those who differed too noticeably. But Amherst, however conservative, was also founded at a time when America was changing decisively. Within the first decade, our curriculum was subject to repeated criticisms. It was too narrow; there wasn't enough science in it; we taught

Latin and Greek but no modern languages. For a brief time we experimented with a less classical alternative toward the bachelor of arts degree. But then, in the words of Hugh Hawkins, an eminent historian of higher education, "Amherst retreated completely from curricular innovation." It would take a whole generation before Amherst returned to reform and choice in the curriculum. Nonetheless, the criticisms seem to have gradually and almost silently moved us to accept European languages and more and more serious science. You could not have a first-rate faculty without dissent and criticism and eagerness to push on with new ideas and new disciplines. Physical education was organized and required at Amherst long before other colleges did so. Chapel was required long after.

Gradually the ideal of the pious man gave way before the more secular vision of "the whole man." This vague American blend of the Protestant Christian, the Roman citizen and the Renaissance classicist was to bewitch this and other colleges for more than a century, well beyond the disillusionments of the First World War. It justified many requirements and impositions, and no doubt many prejudices. But above all it justified the college's stubborn resistance to wide-open inquiry, by students and faculty. In its own way it was a new piety, a new orthodoxy.

Yet it had the distinct advantage of allowing, and even inviting, its own eventual subversion.

The years after the Civil War witnessed America's economic and geographic emergence as an expansionist world power. Across this land, colleges and universities were founded, private and public, small and large. Women were beginning to be educated, first in this valley, over at Mount Holyoke, and then in New England, and then everywhere. The black colleges were founded and flourished, despite poverty and racism. Universities emerged from colleges. Graduate schools were created and doctorates conferred. Specialization was all the rage on faculties, including ours.

Naturally, Amherst resisted some of this. It resisted curricular reform, it resisted expansion into a university, but more to the point Amherst resisted the surrender of its sense of itself and its purposes. To this resistance we owe our greatest strength and distinction, our commitment to undergraduates.

Many at the turn of the century—including many Amherst graduates—predicted the death of the liberal arts college. It would go down as a silly anachronism, a provincial and inadequate little holdout against the superiority of the universities. Others held on more fiercely than ever to ideals of the close relation between scholar and student, ancient ideals that we see most vividly in Plato's writings about Socrates.

It was in these crucial years as we began the twentieth century that Amherst quietly embraced choice for undergraduates. It was an inescapable reform: many of our faculty had Ph.D.s, from the German universities or Johns Hopkins or Harvard, places that took specialization seriously; the sheer number of disciplines made knowing a little of everything silly and, more and more obviously, either narrow or superficial. At Harvard, Charles William Eliot had led a kind of academic coup that gave him the power to impose his vision on not only the students and faculty but the corporation as well. He served forty years as president, from 1869 to 1909, and everywhere preached the gospel of elective study and free inquiry.

Amherst scholars have done as much research on this period as anyone, not only Hugh Hawkins, in his magnificent book *Between Harvard and America: The Educational Leadership of Charles W. Eliot,* but many others, most recently professor of English Kim Townsend, whose *Manhood at Harvard,* published in 1996, probes the ideology of masculinity and identity in this period of American history.

At Amherst itself, first seniors and then juniors and finally sophomores and freshmen were allowed to "elect" sciences and languages and other courses. Professor Hawkins reports that around the turn of the century Amherst students could choose most of their courses. We had no majors in place then, no requirement of courses to be chosen across the disciplines, and only a few reliclike required courses for all to take in time for graduation. Those were the days to yearn for.

Then, as often happens, the alumni got into the act. In a notorious report in 1910, they attacked the free Amherst curriculum as lax and undisciplined. Within two years, Amherst, like Harvard under Eliot's successor at the very same time, had a kind of counter-reformation under way. Alexander Meiklejohn, a truly distinguished First Amendment scholar, became Amherst's president and espoused what he argued was a "balanced" set of requirements, emphasizing the humanities and philosophy in particular as the core disciplines of Amherst's curriculum. An odd compound of radical and conservative in curricular as well as constitutional debates, Meiklejohn wanted something of a return to the "whole man" period. But his was a more intellectual and certainly less religious vision of the liberal arts at Amherst. Meiklejohn was an impatient and brooding man, as well as a beguiling one. Despite his eloquence, he never gained the power with the faculty or the Board to put his vision fully in place. Yet in a sense he triumphed over those committed to choice and electives.

Over many years, the Amherst faculty gradually amended the curriculum with requirements. First, at the alumni's suggestion, they required science and languages. Then later, they divided the curriculum into the famously inexact three divisions—the humanities, the sciences, the social sciences—and required students to take some of each. This so-called distribution requirement is now a feature of virtually every curriculum on every campus save the few, like ours, that have returned to what was once called electivism.

In the late '40s and early '50s, an extraordinary group of faculty, headed by a professor of philosophy named Gail Kennedy, created a new curriculum at Amherst. It adopted Meiklejohn's idea of a junior and senior college experience and imposed its requirements on the first two years. By this time, majors were *de rigueur* everywhere in America, a quiet and universal reform that remains unquestioned still as another century closes.

The new curriculum received national attention for its rigor and inventiveness. Students reading about it now—and indeed alumni recalling it to memory—emphasize, naturally enough, its requirements. On arriving at Amherst, the freshman student was enrolled in a curriculum that left him almost no choices for the better part of two years. The entering student at Amherst was enrolled in three separate sequences in both semesters of the first and second years: Science 1 and 2, emphasizing physics and math; Humanities 1 and 2, focused on Western European history; and, perhaps most important, English 1 and 2, the then well established creation of

Professor Theodore Baird in English, a kind of crusty, local Socratic genius who taught often without readings or books and who may be the greatest teacher that Amherst has ever known.

Baird had come to the college in the '20s and not long after began to develop his writing course. He would put nearly impossible questions to a couple of generations: "Describe what it is like to be angry without saying anything about what made you angry." "Draw a picture of the Holyoke Range. Now tell me what you did, but don't tell me that you drew a picture of the Holyoke Range." For a time, a long time, the English Department (and in some sense the whole faculty) was in the intellectual thrall of this man (some of whose writings professor William Pritchard has edited in a book, *The Most of It*). The New Curriculum was not really new, even at the start: it was at least as old as Baird's career at Amherst. He had dissented sharply from the loose generalizations and pieties of the curricular thinking of the '30s. Finally, in Gail Kennedy's deft work, the entire curriculum was remade on the template of English 1.

It is an important template even now at Amherst, if a dramatically simple one. When you read Kennedy's rambling book about the New Curriculum, called *Education at Amherst: The New Program,* you come away with the sense that no one has ever quite said what is going on in the reform, what it is that was improved upon with the new requirements and the new courses. Kennedy and his colleagues on the long-range planning committee repeatedly quote the American philosopher John Dewey on "learning by doing." They speak of "laboratory courses" in various subjects, but give no exact definition or concrete examples of what they had in mind with this image.

When you speak with Amherst faculty colleagues of theirs, and with the alumni who were their students, you get a somewhat different impression of their particular interpretation of Dewey's famous educational pragmatism. Dewey and Whitehead and the other pragmatists had their greatest influence on primary and secondary schools, where learning by doing meant field trips and experiments and exercises of various kinds. Some of that undoubtedly crept into the Amherst curriculum during this ferment. But the distinctive transition in the New Curriculum was toward a more specific version of learning by doing, Baird's kind, I think: learning, that is, by writing. It was not new, I think, even when Baird joined the faculty in 1927 or Robert Frost in 1917. If anyone deserves credit for its intense usage as a tool of learning and teaching, it is Baird himself; but he gave the credit to Frost. In Robert Frost's teaching there was a startling emphasis on words and their sounds. "As for me," he once said, "I side with those who do something, like playing a game to win or writing a poem."

This is perhaps the most fundamental curricular commitment of any liberal arts college. If you can think it, you can say it; and if you can say it, you can write it.

Coming from high school, you may still associate this discipline with English classes. That is an example of an important fallacy, the fallacy of localizing what you have just discovered; of failing, that is, to generalize it and understand how widespread it may be. I met up with it in a certain place, and so that's the only place it exists. Here you will find that good writing—good explaining—is prized not just in literature classes but more or less everywhere: in the studio, the laboratory, the radio station—and, yes, even in the administration. In the sciences, in the arts, in the humanities and the social sciences, many of us on the faculty believe most deeply in learning by writing. Careful, articulate, often surprising writing is the real mark of the distinctive culture of the liberal arts. Yes, we talk and argue, almost ceaselessly. And we read whatever we can get our hands on. We paint and we sculpt and make films. But in the end people write: our faculty writes and our students write and our graduates write. And after a while—not after four years necessarily, but perhaps six or eight or ten—people tend to write fairly well. This is the real course here, a course in writing as the first and fundamental discipline of thinking and imagining.

If Warhol was right when he said that each of us gets fifteen minutes of celebrity, then a corollary may be that each curriculum gets a run of twenty or thirty years. The New Curriculum at Amherst was soon the old curriculum. New faculty did not relish teaching courses devised by others and imposed on them and their students. Science 1, English, and the other courses—all required passion and could not simply be passed to those who did not really believe in them. And so Amherst, starting around 1966, dismantled our old curriculum and its elaborate structure of requirements. First, there was a new course for first-year students called Problems of Inquiry; and later, there was the Introduction to Liberal Studies, team taught by professors from different disciplines. It took on great themes or concepts, such as the nature of light or the concept of evolution. But this course evolved as well: team teaching was not always practical; professors wanted to offer the seminars on their own, on subjects of their own choosing and design. As recently as two years ago, the faculty recognized both the importance of first-year seminars—small courses exclusively enrolling first-semester students—and the need to open up the scope of faculty choices in designing these courses. And the overall structure has evolved as well. Thus, over decades, even as we have imposed fewer and fewer general requirements, our departments and programs have continued to strengthen the majors with new structures and new requirements.

Moreover, no account of Amherst's curriculum would make sense without acknowledging how much we have changed the offerings themselves with new disciplines and interdisciplinary programs. We realized, too slowly, how for more than a century we had dismissed the imagination and the arts in our commitment to reasoning and explaining. Similarly, if earlier, we realized how much of the world we ignored in seeing ourselves exclusively as heirs of Europe's culture and Europe's institutions. We now seek to embrace in our curriculum as much of the world's experience as we can know and teach, and as many of the arts as we can hold in our small college.

"So what?" Baird might have said. How does all this touch you who have only just begun? Let me make a small effort to include you in this not-so-local history. The shifts at Amherst—between choice and structure, between depth and breadth—have caught up with you, and with all of us, at an odd angle to the prevailing wisdom. Some twenty or thirty years ago the demands for curricular choice (and all sorts of other choices as well) reached a crescendo. Many, many colleges opened up their curricula to student choices. I say many;

not all, and none that I know of all the way. No college in America granted or grants degrees to those who have not accepted structure that was unknown a century ago. This is true—and grows more true of us—as you and we put so much emphasis on the majors. But the historical terrain ought to be unmistakable: very few colleges in America allow as much choice to students as Amherst. Even Brown, the Jacobin revolutionary in this, whose curriculum is said to have been designed by a student—albeit one long passed on into wealth, notoriety, and middle age—even Brown now proposes a required course in ethics in addition to the major requirement. And we at Amherst have consistently required some variant on the freshman seminars that you are now enrolled in. But the point remains: you have much more freedom of choice in what you study here than your colleagues at other institutions around the country and indeed the world.

You have had sermons aplenty on making a responsible use of your freedom. I will add only this. Camus said that after forty your face is your own responsibility. Your mind becomes your own much sooner than that, much sooner than even twenty, I should guess. So I say to you that now, here and from now on, your mind is your own. Your intellectual development depends less on us than on you.

This is perhaps always true, whatever the requirements of a given setting or institution. But you are here for a reason. You are here because you choose to become not just someone with a degree and courses behind you, but an *intellectual*: someone for whom ideas, the push and pull and play of ideas, are powerful and interesting and, above all, unintimidating. Issues of freedom and structure, of depth and breadth, haunt all intellectual life at age sixteen or sixty, in 600 B.C. as much as 2000 A.D. The difference is that now, here at college but more to the point here in you, you must take on these issues—with guidance, with structure, but with a remarkable range of choice. College may seem to mark a kind of high point in your lives as intellectuals. The choices before you must seem nearly infinite. But this is only the beginning of your freedom and your exploration.

Students and Scholars

When I first studied philosophy, I read Aristotle's *Poetics* and *Politics*, as many of you will in introductory courses. I was moved by the sweep and power of some of the definitions that Aristotle offered: "Tragedy," he wrote, "is the mimesis, the imitation, of an action that is passionate and complete and has greatness in it, with words that give pleasure . . . showing what is done and not telling of it, through pity and fear inspiring the catharsis, the purification, of these and other like emotions. . . ." In the *Politics* he defined the Greek city-state, the *polis*, as "a community of families and settlements in a complete and separate way of life . . . in order to live together happily and nobly." This last phrase was a portion of his insistence that politics and government concern themselves with the ends and not just the means of living.

In a very few words, definitions of this sort seem to tell us truths about ourselves and our lives together, truths familiar in some sense but difficult to capture.

A definition like Aristotle's seeks to set down the most important features of a complex activity like a city-state or a drama. It is by its very nature an interpretation: a view or opinion, that is, subject to criticism and competition from other interpretations. The best of these accounts or definitions may well draw the sharpest challenges.

I'd like to ask about the definition of a college, and in particular about the relationship between what most of us see as its central activities: teaching and scholarship. In raising this question, I am asking a kind of moral question about what a college stands for, here and now. In characterizing it, each of us participates in an argument that turns back on itself: any college is what a classicist once called an "essentially contested concept," one that is inherently controversial; a college at its best is an essentially contested institution. Its nature is to elicit dispute and argument, even over its own identity.

My own simplest statement of what we are about is this: we are a gathering of students and scholars for the sake of learning. I admit a mild evasion in the generality of these terms. This is America; these are undergraduates in pursuit of degrees that lead on to careers; the ideology of the liberal arts is itself a part of larger, often unstated, ideology about careers for the leadership class in our society. Nonetheless, I come back to what seems to me fundamental and defining: we gather here as students with the scholars who are our teachers; all the rest is secondary or complementary—the dorms, the library, the laboratories, the theaters, the meals, the schedule, even, in a sense, the curriculum.

The most generally controversial feature of this very simple definition is the insistence that the teachers at a college—the faculty—should be scholars. Or, to put this fairly, the controversy centers around the *balance* between the commitment to scholarship and the commitment to teaching.

Critics, including alumni, make the point that teaching is what is essential in a liberal arts college. To them, scholarship is secondary, and certainly not of the essence. So it is important that we restate and re-argue our conception of the importance of scholarship in what we are and what we do.

Most of us will acknowledge the primacy of teaching. We are not gathered—we were never gathered—solely to do research together, as a simple academy, a pure research institution. Research was never our reason for being: our founders did not think so; our supporters do not think so now. Educating is our chief purpose and has been so from the beginning.

Yet we touch on a real ambiguity in this. Study is an end in itself, much of the time. Indeed, where we cannot treat it as an end, we will often reduce it to the crassest of means—to a good grade or a good résumé or a good job. And where we reduce our study in this way to some immediate end, we will lose at least a portion of the joy and reward of inquiry. The negative way in which we define the liberal arts—as *not* being vocational or immediately applicable—is a roundabout way of insisting on the importance of study as an end in itself. You may intend to be an inventor or an executive and bend many of your day-to-day efforts to this purpose. But your most glorious moments in the physics laboratory will not be those that fall neatly into line as leading on to your vocation. To the contrary, they will be those moments in which the excitement of learning and discovering brings you a joy that stands alone.

If I am even partly right about the joys of study in the lives of students, then we come face to face with the paradox that the best study—and thus presumably the best teaching—occurs when the student becomes a researcher, that is, someone motivated by curiosity and the quest to know, rather than by some need to learn one thing in order to do or accomplish another. In this sense, as in the language of the medieval universities, students and professors here are scholars together, studying together in a joint enterprise, with the professors situated much farther down the road of study and research, but on the same road and with the same purpose and direction.

Great teaching is itself a kind of mystery. Dostoyevsky has Alyosha Karamazov smile skeptically at the bold assertions of a fourteen-year-old who suddenly realizes, under the influence of just that smile, how much he has to learn. In one of the many beautiful images of teaching that Plato, the student, attached to his memory of Socrates, his teacher, a spark jumps from one soul to another at the moment of learning, igniting the same fire, with the same brightness and warmth in both. A faculty member told me once of his own joy in the student who wrote on her exam paper of her reaction to Nabokov: "I'm in love with the sentences," she said, "faltering, tripping over my words, only able to choke forth these few."

I want to approach the question of the balance of teaching and scholarship in the spirit of these images and impressions: we are all students and, in a sense, we are all teachers. What we have in common—what we must have in common—is an attitude toward our common work that I will call scholarly. It shapes a vocation for the faculty; it shapes four years for undergraduates; for all of us it shapes our lives, whatever vocation we may take up later on.

Critics, too, have emphasized questions of attitude or motivation. Critics as far back as the Greeks have attacked the bad attitudes of students, seen as idlers and dilettantes, carousing and cutting classes, more interested in romance than study. Aristophanes went after Socrates and the other teachers of his period as distractedly and absurdly intellectual and occasionally corrupt. The present critique is in this sense in an old tradition in which the leisure time that is required for scholarshipis seen as wasted or at least frittered away.

The harshest critics have treated scholarship as a professorial indulgence. In the classic form of the criticism, which appears in the *Wall Street Journal* more or less weekly, an arcane or silly example of scholarly work is trotted out for an editorial thrashing. And once the thrashing is administered, the journalistic taskmaster smacks his or her lips in satisfaction, pronounces either all or most scholarship *worthless,* and then tells us colleges and universities to get back to our real work in the classrooms. *Some* of what passes for scholarship in this country and others *is* silly; of course it is. Socrates was a constant critic of the Sophists; we too must take on the sophistry of our own culture, including the sophistry of the academy. But that is a small concession to a sweeping critique.

Implicitly, these harsh critics suggest three kinds of faculties or faculty members. The first is the faculty member for whom teaching holds no interest and research is the true and exclusive vocation. Most of us have known great scholars of this sort. They are happiest in research institutes, or at least in the graduate schools of universities. A college is not the right place for such a person, and no one on the faculty believes that it is or should be. So on this first model the critics have no quarrel with us. But the critics' real target is the faculty member whom we do take for a model, the one for whom teaching and research make a joint vocation. Now individual faculty members, on any faculty, will differ in their motivations, and differ, too, at different points in their own lives. There will inevitably be periods of doubt about research or teaching, or both, in the lives of our best and most interesting professors. But I would be hard put to find any great college professor whom I would hesitate to describe as a scholar. And there is no one on a good college faculty who does not see herself or himself as a teacher.

Still, harsh critics say that we are kidding ourselves, and wasting time and effort by doing so. They condemn the scholar-teacher as a pious fraud. They would style us all teachers, first and last. I assume they would want to hold on to the adjective "scholarly," but they want little or no scholarship to go with it. I should be clear here that when we use the word *scholarship*, we mean the full range of a scholar's work and expression. We are proud to count artists as faculty members—poets, novelists, composers, actors, directors, singers, painters, sculptors. Their work helps us all to see that what matters is not so much the form or quantity of the work, but its expressiveness, its originality and incisiveness; its truthfulness. To put this plainly, we take pride in *all* of our faculty. We don't count pages or canvases or productions. We have Socrateses among us who rarely publish, and Aristotles who publish volumes. But the college itself is a kind of public square, a place where ideas are set out to be tested and tried, in classrooms, lectures, arguments, demonstrations, journals, books, exhibits, performances. Ultimately, in whatever form we publish, we make our ideas public as Socrates did, by presenting them to an audience that we can challenge and that can challenge us in return.

Now the teachers our harsh critics hold up as models have put aside research; it is secondary to what they really do; they teach first and foremost—

they teach because the young need to learn and because *they* know what the young should know.

All of us may have known teachers who fit this description to an extent: where the subjects are simple and well bounded; where the knowledge in question is unvarying; and where controversy over methods and conclusions is rare or unacknowledged. Reading seems to have once been taught this way. Assume, for the sake of this argument, that there *are* teachers—good teachers—who teach what they know and have no active interest in knowing more.

The question then becomes: what subjects and at what level might these teachers teach? (I leave aside the question of whether we can believe that the lack of scholarly interest *improves* their teaching.) Surely there are no subjects taught at the level of a liberal arts college or university that quite fit the bill.

My own experience, as early as I can remember, was of good or great teachers whose modesty was such that they always pointed to the unknown, even as they taught what they *did* know. Their own curiosity was eager and vivid. They were good teachers because they were good students, abidingly, actively, demandingly.

I want to argue above all for a disposition to scholarship, a vocation for it. I assert a quality and not a quantity. In colleges and universities, there is no formula by which to predict the precise balance of passions and achievements in a lifelong vocation. But the scholarly interest is always alive and active in the best teachers. I can't find the seam where the lives of college faculty divide into scholar on the one hand and teacher on the other. These critics then are wrong. In their eagerness to condemn, they dismiss the very qualities that animate great teaching and make it possible.

A gentler version of the critique might accept what I have argued and yet still criticize us for a lack of balance in the way we work. Some of the most loyal alumni wonder if we have kept the right balance between scholarship and teaching. Some of our most successful faculty, on the other hand, worry that we lean sometimes too hard toward teaching.

The controversy goes to the heart of our work and vocation. Needless to say, Socrates never faced the question we face every day: do we give more time to teaching or more to the scholarship by which we ourselves, as faculty, learn and advance learning? Our junior faculty, in particular, feel this question in the rounds of their professional lives. But in the lives of all our faculty, the press of time forces choices that often present themselves as a simple divide: teaching versus research.

I will resort to what I take to be a scholarly (and certainly a Socratic) virtue in saying that we can never be sure that we *have* kept the right balance. Not every college has strong scholarly ambitions, we know that much; few liberal arts colleges have faculties that compare with the best universities in the quality and even the quantity of the faculty's scholarship. Few have teaching loads and sabbatical policies as generous toward scholarship. Nonetheless, the best colleges do devote great resources to scholarship. Yet the colleges seem again and again to recruit faculty for whom teaching is central. Those few faculty who leave for universities will often say that they do so "for graduate students" or "for more time for research," implying that the tilt toward research is what prompts them to go. The great universities have entrusted much of *their* teaching to graduate students. We colleges entrust essentially none of it to anyone but our own faculty.

Our ideal is plain: we seek to create here a gathering of students and scholars that can offer the best undergraduate education in the world. A system of teaching assistants cannot, I think, be defended under that ideal. If, as I said at the outset, the question of the balance between teaching and scholarship is a moral one, then we should be clear about the moral nature of the struggle to maintain the balance in our lives and the life of the college.

The balance has to unite the scholarly virtues with those of teaching, as I believe it does. The deeply moral nature of teaching hardly needs to be explained. The relation is second only to parent and child in its trust: that the learning sought and offered will be genuine and not sophistical or fraudulent; that it will challenge the intellect and will of the student; and that it will give the intellectual foundation on which to build a fulfilling life.

By contrast, the moral nature of scholarship is often reduced to simple honesty about sources and authorities. In most discussions, it comes down to what one of my first law professor colleagues used to call "the morality of the footnote."

I join him in saying that the arguably vanishing footnote does, indeed, have a morality in it, if often concealed in the excesses to which it tempts us. The footnote says that your own conclusions have been compared with those of others who have studied the same materials. It points the reader toward the work of those who may have helped you find your way (and away from those who might lead you astray). It says to the reader, "Go. See for yourself." This is a teaching virtue, I think, and suggests again the tie between teaching and scholarship.

But I would argue that the morality of our enterprise rests most fundamentally on a deeper moral structure inherent in the idea of scholarship.

Putting aside skills and facts, what should a student learn at college? My answer is that the student who learns the way of the scholar, who learns to practice it, if only for a short time, has learned all that we could hope to teach were she to stay a century. The scholar is one who pays close attention to a subject; and close attention—attentiveness—is, in a profound sense, the first moral virtue. Only by opening our eyes can we open our hearts. Simone Weil, the French mystic, spoke of attentiveness as the purest form of love on earth. Plato had it that the philosopher, the lover of wisdom, is one stopped in his tracks by wonder; the scholar pursues wonder and seeks to find its source. Scholarly inquiry disciplines our curiosity and leads it on to knowledge. Even more, disciplined inquiry leads the scholar on to inquire yet further, to ask more questions, and to see that knowledge itself is always alive with new questions and the possibility of new insight and revised conclusions.

The scholar must have, as well, the courage of convictions, the courage to teach them, to put them forward in whatever form best expresses them, whether in the classroom, lectures, performances, books, essays, paintings, poems. This was once a college structured by religious faith. Now we embrace less certainty and more doubt. Yet we remain "a city on a hill," one to which young and old come to inquire about the truth. It may seem an unruly, even anarchic city at times; certainly it is an unpredictable one. That too is part of its greatness. The college depends for its order and strength on the balance we strike every day, all of us, between the two great passions that have brought us together—the passion to teach and the passion to learn. In the oldest sense of the word, then, it remains a *school*, a place, that is, to share in the rigors and joys of scholarship.

The Freshman Who Hated Socrates

I had a student one fall who hated Socrates. Week after week he would take up his place around the circle of chairs squeezed into my office: "The man's a fool," he would write in his weekly paper. "He has no compassion for the people he questions." "He makes no sense." Whatever we read, it was the same: in Aristophanes, in Xenophon, in Plato, Socrates was overbearing, petulant, silly, cruel. I tried by comments and questions to bring out the nuance and depth of these opinions. I made little progress: "I hate this guy; I have no respect for him." Why do you hate him? "I don't know, I just do." I was frustrated, and at a loss as to how to teach through this distaste to some appreciation of what he wanted to dismiss.

What I realized as I went on teaching was that I was prepared to compass any indictment or dismissal of Socrates by my freshman if only he were prepared to argue. By the time we were a few weeks into the semester, I didn't care a bit if he liked Socrates or hated him. I just wanted him to construct a case against Socrates, a case with evidence, some charges, and a chain of reasoning leading to his conclusion.

We say we teach the liberal arts, the liberating or freeing arts. Yet we recognize, with Socrates, that we must in some sense force our students to free themselves. *"On les forcera d'être libres,"* Rousseau wrote: we will force them to be free. Few of us subscribe to Rousseau's political philosophy in this respect. Force is much too strong a word for this context of ours, where students apply to college and then choose to enroll. Still, we who teach the liberal arts recognize the sometimes illiberal forces that bring us our students and keep them at their desks. We know we must strike a balance between their choices for themselves and our choices for them. My thesis here is that we will have a much clearer view of our purposes and achievements in the liberal arts if we acknowledge the constraints upon our students, constraints of many kinds, some imposed by us as we fashion a curriculum for them and some carried by them as they make their way to and through college toward lives of their own design.

I want to avoid in this discussion the easy extremes. There is the view, on the one hand, that since students choose a particular college they cannot complain of its coercions or constraints. In constitutional law this view has come to be called taking the bitter with the sweet. In my view, our students have standing to complain of too much constraint even if they have contracted with us for the services we offer. On the other hand, there is the view that the student must be left to roam among our offerings like a shopper with a cart, picking here and there the items she wants. Anything less, this view holds, infringes the free choice of the student, whose maturity is not to be questioned. I have tried out this particular vision, as you will hear, and I cannot say that it worked.

But let me return to my freshman.

The freshman who hated Socrates at first resisted every effort to make him argue his case. Did he do so out of cunning? Did he know in some way that to argue in the way I wanted was to succumb, to fall into a trap? To dismiss Socrates outright, without nuance or argument, was to have nothing to do with him. Whereas to dismiss him with arguments—by meeting this point and refuting that—was to entangle oneself in a Socratic web of arguments leading to the goal of a liberally educated person, someone who would reject no serious opinion without inquiry and reflection.

Courses, like cultures, move on from question to question, not so much because they have settled anything as because they find something else more interesting. So my freshman moved on. Did he come to respect Socrates at last? I cannot say for sure; he did begin to argue with him. We turned to other subjects and let Socrates go.

My course was a freshman seminar. The hope is that every freshman will take one. Why did he take my seminar, called Socrates Citizen? Perhaps he anticipated something very different from what I taught; perhaps he wanted to see what the president of the college was about; perhaps he thought Socrates was a kindly old man. One of the most famous commentators on Plato's *Republic* recalled that he studied Greek because, as a boy in a village in Scotland, he once saw Greek letters at school and loved the shape of them.

My student may help us to think about the balance in our liberal arts curriculum between constraint and freedom.

When I went from teaching law to teaching philosophy, I felt that the change was not so very great. I had gone into teaching after a short stint in a bilingual grammar school in Boston. "Teaching is pretty much the same," I used to say, "whether it's kindergarten or graduate school." In law school I taught philosophy of law and ethics, among other things. I teach the same subjects now in college. The continuity in teaching these ideas conceals a shift in the context and ambition of the two institutions. I only later began to feel the full force of the change.

The institutional ends of a law teacher are as various as any other teacher's, I am sure. Yet there is an important sense in which all law teachers greet their students with the same ambition. Law teachers, whatever else they do, teach their students to become lawyers. Among other things, they must hope they will pass the bar exam.

How do liberal arts teachers greet their students in this sense? What do we teach them to become? We teach in various disciplines, but all to the same end, we say. The idea behind our teaching, the ambition in it, is larger than in a professional school: we teach the liberal arts, the arts that are supposed to *liberate* our students (and surely ourselves as well). But how are our students to become free? Our rhetoric suggests that *these* studies, in *these* disciplines, have a particular power to liberate. But why? We should be wary of the seductiveness of our own rhetoric.

In what was for me the most memorable lecture of my own college days, the philosopher Hannah Arendt warned a crowd of late-'60s students against overly abstract ideals: "The more distant the ideal is from realization," she said, "the more dangerous it is." Surely she was right. The more vast the ideal, the more general, the more it would seem to justify and excuse. Distant freedoms may seem to justify present coercions. Bertolt Brecht spoke of the necessity of building a gentler society by ungentle means. No doubt coercion and even violence may be necessary and justifiable in the achievement of certain political ideals. But when the ideal is far distant, in time or in conception, we can sometimes delude ourselves that we move toward it, when in fact the ground shifts under us and we make no advance.

To say that we teach in order to free, to liberate, is to voice a proposition that we will have trouble testing.

We should be very explicit, then, about what we hope to achieve. The obstacles we face could not be more concrete, or more unyielding. Take the career anxieties of our undergraduates as just one example. What can we do about them and the ways in which they constrain students' choices? A senior asked me how to explain to a bank interviewer that majoring in religion was a helpful endeavor. We might hope, I suppose, to abolish such anxieties, and to liberate undergraduates from all concern about where they will go and what they will do when they have done with us. A more realistic approach is to harness these anxieties, to channel them (and challenge them) in studies that will prove helpful to the ambitions of students yet are much more than stepping stones to jobs or a profession. What exactly do we mean by freedom in this context of the liberal arts? The simplest answer comes to us by way of classical political philosophy. The freedom we seek for our students—*with* our students—is the freedom suited to and necessary for citizenship in a free society. This is the concept of the liberal arts. But this translation, like the original, remains vague.

We must ask, Free in what sense, free *from* what, and free *to* what? A free citizen is free to participate in a free society. This freedom, while vital, is narrow, because politics must be narrow, focused. It justifies only a few elements of our curriculum. It leaves out—or tempts us to leave out—the arts, poetry, the sciences, and much else. And it does not suggest much about the structure, and the ideal, with which we confront the freshman who hated Socrates. What *are* the coercions or constraints that confront him, and how do they contribute to his ultimate freedom?

Let me state three ideals that I would tie to the ambitions of the liberal arts: First, it is our ambition, so far as possible, to free our students and ourselves from all manner of prejudice. By "prejudice" I mean something much broader than racial or sexual biases. I mean *judgment in advance* of persons or ideas: rash, unthinking conviction, held against evidence and without discussion, without inquiry or reflection. Prejudice of this sort comes as naturally as breathing. The human mind is made to have opinions, and, it seems, to have them in a hurry. It is a lifelong commitment to free one's opinions of prejudice, a lifelong study. Our efforts should provide a foundation for that effort.

The second liberating ambition of the liberal arts is more difficult to capture in a few words. It has to do with the intellectual and moral confidence of our students, and with their sense of the possibilities of knowledge and the usefulness of inquiry. The narrowness of any merely *political* statement of "freedom to" is palpable for most of us when we think of the range of students we have taught, budding poets and philosophers and physicists and even monks. Socrates himself, according to Libanius, was accused of uninvolvement in civic matters. We would have our students grow in the mastery of certain subjects; that is plain. We insist on what we take to be the breadth and rigor of the disciplines we teach as the liberal arts. Somewhere in these efforts lies a conviction that our students will come to believe in the power—the liberating power—of study, and of inquiry generally. There is a liberation in that confidence because it frees them to approach others, to approach the world, and to approach their own lives in the spirit of inquiry. In that spirit, they will learn to be confident not so much of their answers as of their questions.

The third ambition I would mention is related to the second. Over this century, American colleges and universities have come to rely on the major, a subject in which a student concentrates much of her attention, particularly in the last two years of study. I suspect that there are many reasons for our reliance on majors, some only distantly tied to this question of freedom. The major may be the most notable constraint we place on our students. The liberating ambition in it seems to me this: no one mind can encompass all the world; each of us has to focus somehow; the study of one discipline leads us toward mastery. We cannot put too fine a point on the mastery of an undergraduate, you may say, wisely. But the rigor of our majors does in fact require our students to focus on certain techniques and approaches, on one body of knowledge, as against others. This constraint of focus brings with it, in virtually every case, an understanding of a discipline much beyond that of the dilettante or dabbler. Concentration is freeing, in the hard way that craftsmanship frees. The person who knows one discipline well knows the world well, too, if only through that one lens. And the person who knows no discipline well, however sophisticated or well informed, lacks an essential tool of understanding and mastery.

A curriculum, then, a liberating curriculum, should, first, challenge its students in such a way as to shake them free of the habits of prejudice; second, it should make them confident of their own (and of others') powers of inquiry and understanding; and third, it should provide an apprentice's understanding of one of the great disciplines that make up the loose collection of disciplines we call the liberal arts.

Perhaps none of us is as free as we imagine ourselves. William James once remarked that we view nearly everything we ourselves do as freely chosen and nearly everything our neighbor does as the product of his history and environment. Constraints of all kinds meet us in all that we do, and certainly in our teaching.

One of the chief constraints in teaching—one that Socrates battled in the effort to distinguish himself from the Sophists, who could teach you to triumph over rivals in the courtroom or the marketplace—is what the students themselves seek from their educations. No less than law schools, we give our students a credential. In this, as in virtually all other societies, higher education positions graduates in a structure of expectation and performance, of power and class. Those with higher education will likely have more to say about the direction and pace of our institutions. They will have higher and more strategic positions. Our degrees qualify our students for jobs or for further schooling leading to jobs. In all of this there is a structure of peer and parental expectation that doing such a degree is normal, is part of growing up, is what nearly everyone else of similar ability and ambition is doing at this stage of life.

Were we to proceed in our academy as Plato did in his, were we to offer no degrees, we would have very few students. Students come to us for the liberal arts, yes, but most of our students would not come were we to offer nothing in the way of credentials. All colleges and universities do this. We work in and through this constraint.

Freedom in this context begins to look more modest than when I say we teach the liberating arts. Surely, if the liberation were as radical as our rhetoric suggests, we would not have to offer degrees, or give grades, or, for that matter, structure our curriculum so as to steer students into majors and minors in the way we do. I know a religion professor who likes to say that in America the insights of Buddhism are most present amid the rigors of sport. In the America of the liberal arts colleges, too, the insights that constitute freedom must come amid the rigors not only of our teaching but of our society and its pressures on our students.

Take the question of grades and degrees: surely the process of inquiry itself requires neither—one can learn biology or history without being tested and graded, and without the award of a degree. What role do these constraints have in what we do?

The degree means many things in our society. For us, speaking from the inside of the curriculum, it certifies a certain attainment in studies. That attainment has a kind of marketable value in the world at large, one that brings us most of our students. For us, again from the inside of the curriculum, the degree is not so much a constraint as a judgment of attainment. But it does prod our students, in the mass at least, to complete their work. Grades play more or less the same role on the smaller scale of coursework.

"The intellect," wrote George Kennan in his memoir, *Sketches from a Life*, "[is] a lazy, sluggish faculty. Its growth occur[s] only under discipline and discomfort. It [has] to be scourged into the unfolding of its powers." He uses the argument, with only the slightest trace of irony, to make a case against coeducation and in favor of "dark, cold, rainy" locations for universities and colleges. It makes the case for grades more neatly. Were I to press the student who hated Socrates (or math for that matter), I would learn, I believe, that an entirely uncoerced curriculum—without grades or course requirements, degrees or majors and minors—would mean that he never would have done what he did in my seminar, which is to accept the challenge of refuting Socrates rather than simply dismissing him outright. In one of the most poignant and even tragic of Plato's dialogues, the *Gorgias,* Socrates speaks of an interlocutor who spurns discussion and turns away, perhaps forever. "If you refute me," says Socrates, "I shall not be vexed with you as you are with me, but you shall be enrolled as the greatest of my benefactors."

You may well ask what kind of freedom is purchased with such lowly incentives and coercions. It is a good question, and one to which I will give, a little later, a more or less Socratic answer.

Many students, perhaps most students, do not hate Socrates (and, whatever Kennan says, are not lazy). Need we coerce them so vigorously as undergraduates? The argument over minors makes the point forcefully. The most successful minors—I know one on progressive social movements—bring together in a demanding program of study, fieldwork, and writing a group of students who do what they do because they are given the chance, and not because they had to. You could abolish the minors tomorrow and they would still gather with their professors to work on the questions they are passionate about.

There is the germ of an argument here for a curriculum that would harness enthusiasm but never constrain it. Anarchism in curricular matters has a perennial appeal. One professor of philosophy says there is a "genial democracy of achievement" in an open curriculum.

For thirty years, more or less, Brown University has held on to an open curriculum that my friends on its faculty defend in an utterly straightforward way: it brings us better students, they say, brighter, more enthusiastic students, who make more of our teaching and of our curriculum. There is no way for me to test this proposition. The open curriculum remains lively and persuasive too in the memories of many alumni: "I came here for one reason, because of the open curriculum." But we also know that nearly half of open curriculum graduates take no science, that a third take no mathematics, and that nearly a quarter manage to steer clear of all arts courses.

No course of study that I know of is wholly open or unconstrained. We are a small group of teachers, gathered in disciplines, and teaching what *we* know and care about. Our students are all of them constrained by what we know and can teach. We hope they will go much beyond us, past the limits of our knowledge and our techniques. We want them to push their inquiries further than ours.

When I was an undergraduate I took several tutorials. These independent studies went as such courses too often do. The sensation of setting out was exquisite: a whole realm opened up before me and me alone. With just a little help from a professor, I entered into research and reading that was all my own. I remember still the sensation of seeing that a book had not left the library for many, many years, if ever, until I took it out. What I never seemed to realize in time was how slow and inefficient—how lonely—independent research can be. Without a syllabus, without companions, without lectures or discussions, you must blaze your own path. You had better be prepared for it, for the false starts, the tedious readings, the difficulty of finding a vantage point. After three or four tries, I came to feel that some more generous compromise between my own interests and the scarcities of the curriculum was often the wiser choice.

In my senior year, at the tail end of the '60s, we heard from a dean that we could concoct our own courses. Several of us joined in a common venture. I suggested the topic, something about novels of political commitment. Together we recruited a teacher, a wonderfully patient psychoanalyst named Ernst Prelinger. He consented to teach the syllabus we presented. There is no set of readings I remember less well.

What we did not realize in designing our course was that a course looks very different to the student who selects it than to the professor who designs it. The professor will have sifted—painfully at times—through ten times the readings she assigns. To the student, the course will sometimes look like a good excuse for reading Socrates, say, or Gandhi or Dickinson. The professor knows all too well what readings will have to be left out; the student has no idea of this.

I hope I have said enough to convince you of the balance that must obtain—even in an open curriculum—between the student's initiative and the professor's guidance. I draw no simple lesson from this insight.

Ultimately, no curriculum succeeds because of its exquisite architecture; it succeeds because of the faculty and students it brings together. My own undergraduate experiments convince me that we must look to the faculty for the design and shape of any course of study. Its openness to student initiative, to adventures unmapped by the faculty, seems a vital part of its structure. With too much freedom, most students lose their way, as I did briefly; with too little, most lose a sense of enthusiasm—and of an ultimate direction toward freedom.

My own preference is for a gradually loosening structure of guidance, in which students feel themselves more and more at ease and in charge as they advance in the curriculum. That is why I feel that the notion of a core set of requirements fits best at the outset of an undergraduate career in the liberal arts. For a freshman, there should be the exhilaration of choice, but also the guidance of constraint. To say, "You must choose from among this range of courses" seems to me sensible and helpful. To require a small number of core courses seems to me justifiable, so long as those courses are the work of committed and enthusiastic (rather than conscripted) faculty.

Our hesitations about the design of core courses are emblematic of our intellectual situation here and now in America, in liberal arts colleges and universities. To say that all of our students should know *something* of history or politics or literature is easy, so long as we do not say exactly *what* they should know (or in most cases *why* they should know it). Distributional requirements constrain no one less than the faculty (and the deans and presidents) who stand ready to explain and defend them. Is there something liberating in having taken a course here and a course there? Not on the face of it, but I have heard of many students who, prodded by distributional requirements, signed up for courses they would never otherwise have taken. The story is told of an athlete in a dance course who spoke of it as a revelation.

When we turn to the question of a core curriculum, many of us lose much of our confidence in ourselves, and in the constraints we would impose to move our students toward freedom. Our modesty becomes us, in one sense. Few of us nowadays can be accused of arrogance in this discussion. Almost no one on any campus steps forward to say, All of our students must know this or study that. Yes, we can inherit a core,m and maintain it like an old car, adding and adjusting as we go.But we seem unable to create a new core unless it constitutes now and forever an essential acquisition of a liberally educated person. Yet this is to fall into the trap of those whom we criticize for reifying or making permanent their own vision of what students needed to know in the 1920s or '30s. A core does not have to be—and should not be—once and for all.

Freedom in the curriculum stands in balance with constraints of many kinds. The constraints of the curriculum are often counter-constraints, designed to push us all, students and teachers alike, toward the various liberations we seek.

The way for us to embark on the design of a core course is not to ask ourselves what every educated person must know. That inquiry will paralyze and exhaust us. Far better to ask if there are not some themes that we might find helpful and interesting to explore, even if only with next year's freshmen or sophomores. It is no small part of the justification of such courses that they would give us all, for a short time, a common ground on which to argue and inquire. It need not be a permanent acquisition, this common ground. It need not be a local canon or rule. As a constraint, it can be modest, even tentative.

But I think it is nearly always worth a try.

What impresses me most in the undergraduate curriculum of the liberal arts is the way in which students mature to the point of self-direction in their studies. Nowhere is this more striking than in the collaborative laboratory research of some of our senior science majors. It is not that they have eluded supervision, far from it. It is that they have made their way to freedom within a field of study. They have learned to do research within a discipline. They know, in a preliminary way, what their professors do.

Most of us, when we come to college, do not know quite that much. A liberal arts college is a place whose studies and explorations are constrained by an ancient tradition suggesting a distinction between training for usefulness, for employment, and study for living one's life wisely. The distinction is imperfect, we all know. Yet it survives because we continue to find it convincing. We say we do not engage in prevocational, preprofessional studies. A more exact way to say this is to say that while a liberal arts curriculum may function as a prelude to a vocation it is not shaped—and should not allow itself to be shaped—by that function. Whatever our students do when they leave us, we do not prepare them for that first job, or indeed for any job they may hold.

We prepare them for a life of learning and inquiry. To do this, we teach the disciplines that we have found most rigorous and intellectually worthy.

The liberal arts hold out for a freedom that comes with knowledge. Surely knowledge does not in every case win freedom. A broad and comprehensive sense of the disciplines and acquisitions of human culture may accompany many forms of enslavement. But on the whole, nothing prepares us so well for mastery of ourselves and of our own lives as does a knowledge of how others have lived and what truths they have uncovered and what follies they have embraced. The sheer breadth of this task makes the modern liberal arts college and the sprawl of disciplines and inquiries that it is. Somehow, as we shape and reshape this sprawl, we must balance the constraints that order and define our studies with the freedom that we seek through them—and in which we and our students rejoice.

Lear's Wisdom

In the last few weeks, I have been reading and rereading *King Lear,* my favorite Shakespeare play since I was in college. It may be that I have been drawn back to it because of its reverberations in our own era: an era, like Lear's, of rage and catastrophes; an era, too, with its bitter taste of tragic despair.

For all the times that I've read *King Lear,* in school and out, I've seen it on stage only once or twice, and not so memorably as I'd have wished. But I have tapes of a BBC radio production with the late John Gielgud as a roaringly eloquent King Lear. I listened to these tapes as I reread the play. And, like any good student, I read some of the commentary, old and new, by Shakespeare scholars.

An amateur's report on a work of art—the sort of report you will write over and again in class—can never have much authority: this is what I saw and felt, this is what I thought, this is what I learned. Yet works of art derive their powers from effects like these, effects on those of us who come to love them and study them. Few of us can be experts. The ideal of a liberal arts education is that there is something worthy—something essential—in the amateur's experience and reflection. What does one get, what does one learn, from a great play? I'd like to answer that question with a report to you on my own understanding of *King Lear*, a play I love, but with an amateur's affection and not an expert's.

Philosophers since Plato and Aristotle have sought to give very general answers to questions about what art does for us. Aristotle, in particular, reached conclusions that remain satisfying and insightful more than 2,000 years later. Contemporary critics typically seek to understand particular plays or playwrights in the context of a culture, a time, a craft. Amateurs, like me, will necessarily have a more limited sense of the power and beauty of such things as plays, poems, or paintings.

The story of King Lear is simple to tell. An old king decides to retire, thinking to divide his kingdom among his three daughters. At the ceremony of retirement and division, he asks each of them for a declaration of love and gratitude. The two older sisters comply, saying that their father is "all in all" to them. The youngest sister, Cordelia, balks: "How can I heave my heart into my mouth?" she asks. She tells her father the truth, that she loves him as a father, "no more, no less." Enraged, the old king denounces and disowns Cordelia. He then redivides his kingdom between the two older daughters, Goneril and Regan. Cordelia, spurned by her father, is nonetheless taken as wife and queen by the good King of France. There follows a series of confrontations and conspiracies leading on to civil war and disaster: the old king is driven out by the two older sisters, Goneril and Regan, who then turn against each other. Cordelia and her husband bring an army against them, but evil seems to triumph: Lear and Cordelia are imprisoned together.

As if to drive home whatever lessons we may take from this plot, Shakespeare fits it out with a second, shadowing plot: again an old and powerful man, the Earl of Gloucester; again children, this time two sons, one legitimate and the other illegitimate; this time a plan to overthrow the old man, betray the good son, and take the earldom. The bad son, Edmund, who sets out to do this soon has his eye—and more than his eye—on the two sisters and the kingdom as a whole.

In the end, nearly everyone is dead: by murder, suicide, dueling, heartbreak. The two scheming daughters take their own lives. The good brother kills the bad. Cordelia is murdered in prison; her father dies of grief. There is enough blood, betrayal, and sheer badness here for a whole season of *The Sopranos*. It may come to more than one stage can hold of an evening.

Like many others, I find in all this some of the greatest poetry ever written: *King Lear* is shocking, witty, poignant, tragic. It is worth asking why I and so many of us react this way. What makes the words into poetry, and what makes the poetry so powerful?

First, it can't be the *sound* of the words, though there are beautiful sounds throughout the play. Words carry meaning, and the music in them needs, nearly always, to be meaningful to us to be pleasing and, more than pleasing, moving. Second, the poetry must capture feelings, and with feelings settings and scenes that are recognizable to us and powerful to us. And, finally, great poetry will cause us to reflect, to think about what matters most to us and to others, what we should care about and what we should not care about at all.

Take Lear. He is an odd hero in the drama. He is more than eighty years old and often doddering. He is vain, hotheaded, and foolish. Only a reckless fool would divide up a kingdom without a thought to the likelihood of civil war. Only a fool ignorant of his own passions would surrender so much while giving no thought to his own craving for the power he is giving up. Lear has long favored one daughter over the other two, which is a foolish thing in itself. In a blast of anger at his favorite's honesty he thrusts her aside—seemingly forever.

In one of the most powerful exchanges in all of Shakespeare, Lear's loyal and courageous courtier Kent protests all of this: "Check thy hideous rashness," he tells the angry king. Lear shouts him down, but Kent holds his own: "Thou dost evil," he says. In the midst of their argument, Lear seizes on what Shakespeare will make the central metaphor of the play: "Out of my sight," he tells Kent, as he must have told a hundred others before. But Kent defies the king. "*See better,* Lear," Kent says, a striking phrase for an even more striking idea.

We can all see better, always. There is always more to see and learn. And perhaps never in our lives is this advice better given than when we are enraged with those around us, particularly those we love or *have* loved, those who may somehow have hurt us. At those times we miss what should be most present to us, our own deepest wishes for ourselves, for our own good and happiness. In missing these, we can only rarely make out what others wish and need.

In this blindness, this foolishness, of his, Lear is every one of us, perhaps not every day, perhaps not often, but still crucially and dangerously. For Lear, for his mythical Britain, this one act of willful moral blindness leads straight to catastrophe—for him, for his family, for his kingdom. Our own tragedies are never so momentous as this, or so plain to see. Lear's greatness fascinates us and attracts us. Aristotle made it a rule that tragedy required such greatness—precisely so as to hold our attention. But the lesson is the same, writ large or writ small. Moral blindness in the midst of passion, in the midst of crisis, can play havoc with lives.

There are in *King Lear* three casts: first there is the cast of the good, even the saintly. Cordelia is the most notable of these, more eloquent than anyone, even or especially when she is silent, faithful and true in her love right to the end, almost without anger. Her only fault is bluntness, which she may take from her father. Then there is Edgar, the good son of Gloucester. He is patient, steadfast, deeply spiritual, but playful and brave. And there is Kent, less brilliant than Cordelia, less spiritual than Edgar, but the courageous standard bearer of the play's great truths about our moral lives. The second cast is the cast of those who are evil, in most cases more and more evil as the play progresses. The eloquent and ambitious Goneril, the oldest daughter, leads this cast in its scheming, its ambition, its lust. She makes her way from treachery to treachery as a kind of fiend or devil. The next sister, Regan, is no better, though less interesting and less noisy. Most interesting—and noisiest of all—is Edmund, the bastard son of Gloucester. He sneers, laughs, philosophizes, and conspires with wit and gusto.

We hear or watch the play stunned and fascinated by the evil—the daring, uninhibited evil—of this second cast of characters. At one point—as bad as any B movie—Regan presides as her husband jabs out old Gloucester's eyes. When a servant tries to stop them, she kills him with a knife in the back. I laugh to think how the first English crowds must have reacted to this gore.

The good characters in all this are relentlessly good. Shakespeare puts them beyond us, almost from the outset. Cordelia speaks with shocking honesty to her vain old father. Kent defies his lord, risking his life to do so. Only the court jester, the boy who is Lear's fool, seems to have a plausible, near-at-hand goodness, teasing Lear and needling him sarcastically while remaining attached to him and faithful to the end.

But then there is the third cast, of those more like the rest of us, not saints or devils but fallible mortals struggling between good and evil. Gloucester is like this. He is mercurial and gullible, but endearingly decent and courageous. Albany, Goneril's husband, is a minor figure but important in that he moves, gradually but decisively, from evil toward goodness. And, finally, there is Lear himself, who commits the original sin of the play, but then suffers in every possible way as he sputters and declaims and ponders his way toward wisdom, toward "seeing better."

The Tragedy of King Lear may be the greatest play in English, but it is a wild, even grotesque, melodrama, full of calamity and exaggeration. We only *believe* in these characters, we only take them seriously, because of their words. Their words convince us to listen and to watch. Their words speak to us and *for* us. We too have felt these emotions, and we feel them still.

In an artist on canvas it is often the technique that startles and draws our unschooled attention. "Look at this amazing brushwork, that startling deep blue," we say. As we look more, we can begin to see the composition, the art, in this. Whether it is notes of music or forms on canvas or characters on stage, the composition holds our attention and makes us feel and think in ways that the great artist in some way intended.

What kind of composition is Shakespeare's *King Lear*? We must each take from art what we can, provided only that we give it the attention, the study, it requires. For me, *Lear* is a composition about fallibility and wisdom in our lives, the passage from great wrong to something right and true, however sad. In the end, we see better, even if what we see is very sad.

Cordelia seeks to tell the truth about love. She can reason and argue well, and does. But it is her fierce honesty about love that sets her apart and that brings on the wrath of her father. Her love for him was measured and not all consuming, she said. It was better understated than overstated. "Obey you, love you, most honor you," she says to him. But this is not "to love my father *all*." She will soon have a husband and perhaps children, and she will love them too. Love can be shared and must be shared, Shakespeare seems to tell us.

This simple truth might not seem enough to bring down a king, his family, and his kingdom. But Shakespeare never frets too much about the motivation of his characters: Lear's anger, Othello's jealousy, Macbeth's ambition, Hamlet's perplexity—these come before us as forces or facts. They are suddenly in front of us, eloquently and passionately in front of us, and few of us take the time to fret over where exactly they came from. Yes, something is exaggerated or excessive here. Of course it is; it has to be.

What Shakespeare exaggerates is emotion that we all live with, in smaller settings and for smaller stakes, with few or none watching us—hearing us—as we struggle to adjust our judgments and our actions to our passions and furies, to our wants. These in turn are almost always exaggerated, sometimes grotesquely, as we watch a roommate or neighbor obsess over some slight, or as we feel ourselves go round and round about some missed change or other.

Madness has a large place in *King Lear*. Anger itself, as Kent says, is a kind of madness. The king spends much of the play raving on a heath. Gradually, though, he learns his other feelings, mulling them, and reasoning them through. At one point he refuses Kent's offer of shelter in a hovel, saying that he prefers the distractions of the thunderstorm to "the tempest in his mind." He sends Kent into the shelter ahead of him and then turns to the fool, his young jester: "In boy; go first," says the recently all-powerful king. Alone then, outside in the dark, Lear thinks suddenly of all who are too poor to find shelter on this night of rain and wind and thunder:

> Poor naked wretches, whereso'er you are,
> That bide the pelting of this pitiless storm
> How shall your houseless heads and unfed sides,
> Your looped and windowed raggedness, defend you
> From seasons such as these? O, I have ta'en
> Too little care of this!

And then he recommends both reflection and action to those with powers like the ones that once were his:

> Take physic, pomp;
> Expose thyself to feel what wretches feel,
> That thou mayest shake the superflux to them
> And show the heavens more just.

Lear sees here what he had not seen before, and what he had not cared to notice: the sufferings of others, his subjects, not just from rain and cold but also, we guess, from taxation, oppression, war. In the strange-sounding phrase "shake the superflux to them," Lear seems to say that now, in the wilderness, he feels that all that was superfluous and excessive at court should go to his subjects, the poor. It is a thought he will not live to implement, but no matter: we hear him say it, and we are struck by the change in him.

In *King Lear*, Shakespeare tantalizes us with a concluding vision of redemption through love. Lear and Cordelia are captives of the English forces of the two sisters, led by the treacherous Edmund. Cordelia says to her father, "We are not the first who with best meaning have incurred the worst." She wonders if as prisoners she and he will meet up with Goneril and Regan: "Shall we not see these daughters and these sisters?" But Lear is impatient with that forgiving notion. His old anger stirs, and he says: "No, no, no, no!" And then, in an echo of his old possessiveness of Cordelia, he adds: "Come, let's away to prison: [w]e two alone will sing like birds i' the cage." In one of the most beautiful poems in English, he has a vision of happiness in prison with Cordelia: ". . . [s]o we'll live," he says,

> and pray, and sing, and tell old tales, and laugh
> At gilded butterflies, and hear poor rogues

> Talk of court news; and we'll talk with them too,
> Who loses and who wins, who's in, who's out;
> And take upon's the mystery of things,
> As if we were God's spies: and we'll wear out
> In a walled prison, packs and sects of great ones
> That ebb and flow by the moon.

Now, there are many things to say about this vision of Lear's. Some see in it a kind of redemption: at last Lear achieves wisdom—renouncing all the power and intrigue of court for contentment locked away with his beloved daughter in a cell. This is true, I think, but no wisdom comes without its touch of folly. Lear is old and near death; Cordelia is a young bride without children. For her to spend her life in prison in his company would not perhaps be the utopia of renunciation that it might be for her father.

In the end, neither of them reaches anything that I'd call redemption. The play is a tragedy, after all. Samuel Johnson said that for a long time he could not bear to read *Lear* through to the end because of its unspeakable sadness. The great Victorian scholar A. C. Bradley summarized all of Shakespeare's tragedies in a short sentence: "Th[e] central feeling," he wrote, "is the impression of waste." All the beauty, all the greatness, all the intelligence that Shakespeare sets before us, all of it comes to nothing. All of it goes down to destruction—and for no good reason.

In *Lear*, Edmund has given orders that Lear and Cordelia must be killed in prison. But as Edmund dies, after the duel with his brother Edgar, he confesses to his wrongs. "I pant for life," he says,

> some good I mean to do,
> Despite of mine own nature.
> Quickly send,
> Be brief on it, to th' castle;
> For my writ
> Is on the life of Lear and on Cordelia. . . .

In the next scene, Lear carries the dead Cordelia in his arms: "Howl, howl, howl, howl!" Lear says. "She's gone forever. I know when one is dead and when one lives...." He asks for a looking glass—a mirror—to hold up to her lips to see if she still breathes. He imagines for a moment that she does, but she's gone; she's dead.

What is it that Lear sees as he dies?

He sees first how much happiness rests within us, and not without. Wealth and power mean very little up against death. Love, truly felt and truly spoken, love is what counts for most in our lives, as in his.

Second, he sees how important truthfulness is—not just to him and to his daughters, but to his kingdom and to his world. The human world of Shakespeare rises and falls on words truly spoken. Our own world, your world, does as well.

Third, and what may be most important, is what I will call Lear's wisdom: he learns through his own sufferings how much others suffer and how hard we must try to see this, to know it, and to act on it.

In the end, Lear does see better, much better. Like the rest of us, though, he does not see everything. He is neither a saint nor a god. His old possessiveness is still there at the end, chastened and improved. But he sees others at last—not just Cordelia and her sisters, but his subjects, his friends and enemies, his young fool. His last words are like injunctions to us all. "Look there, look there."

Look hard, see well.

Moral Teachers

In my last year in college, I took a seminar on Karl Marx's *Das Kapital*. The professor was a bone-thin young man of wild intensity and seriousness. Often, his wife—who looked to us like his twin sister, equally thin, smart, and unamused—co-taught the course, though she was not listed in the catalogue or on the roster of the economics department. Both were said to be Maoists and members of the Progressive Labor Party, the hardest line of the various small revolutionary parties to be found on campuses in those days.

It was a bizarre assemblage of students for an advanced course in economics: most of us were in philosophy or literature. It seemed that all of us had read nearly everything written by "the young Marx"—because in those days, across the land, every course that touched on the nineteenth century seemed to assign him. There was, as I recall, one initiate among us, a shy young man who wore a suit every day. He was a member of the Communist Party, an alien from the 1930s, and he seemed to all of us like a religious missionary or an insurance salesman who had wandered into the wrong class. Most of the rest of us had never before seen the three thick volumes of *Das Kapital,* published lavishly and cheaply in Moscow. The volumes themselves were in dark blue and deeply embossed, as if they were bound in leather and belonged on the shelves of a collector of first editions.

To us, Karl Marx was a young, trenchant Hegelian, bitter, romantic, aphoristic, a poet of rebellion. The older Marx whom we were to study by way of these volumes remained trenchant and, in his own way, romantic. But the prose was assembled into heavy paragraphs, with charts and statistics gotten up with his collaborator Friedrich Engels. Page upon page of these volumes labor through the specifics of British industrial history to show the workings of capital accumulation and the slow evolution of class consciousness in factory workers. I could not then—and cannot now—say how well done all this research was. Plainly it was research in fealty to an idea, a vision more powerful and animating than any but a very few the world has known for hundreds of years. The work itself is, by almost any standard, deeply eccentric: a hodgepodge of facts and figures thrown together with definite conclusions and passionate conviction. Most of us were ill equipped to understand the work or its author.

Our teacher met with us each week to work through sections of this great work, which to him was a kind of scripture. He took us as he found us, a ragtag group of would-be radicals with no rigorous preparation and a hesitant, mildly skeptical curiosity about a way of thinking that to him was the sun's first light on the very dark night.

I have had funny teachers, warm teachers, brilliant teachers, even mystically inspired teachers; never have I had more intensely passionate and committed teachers than this pair of revolutionaries. I don't know what became of them. My guess is that they are still true believers. I wonder if they still teach.

One day in the spring of 1969, in the minutes before class, they went after a bunch of us for what they took to be the poor quality of our war protests on campus. A large group of us had walked out of the senior dinner because the speaker was McGeorge Bundy, a onetime mathematician and dean, then a leading strategist of the war in Vietnam. I was the one who had seized the American flag, struggling with a security guard over its symbolic ownership, as the group of us marched out of the hall where the dinner was held. (I knew the guard and felt ashamed to have outwrestled a man thirty or forty years my elder. So I surrendered it to him once we were outside on the street. Later I learned that he was cheered when he returned it to the dais.) We had besieged the President's Office, demanding the expulsion of ROTC. But this seemed like paltry exhibitionism to the advocates. "What's going on here?" the two professors asked. "It's not based on any analysis of what can be done, here and now, to end the war and weaken the system. It's an effort to keep up with protests on other campuses, to make sure that this campus is not left behind. It's like a sports rivalry: you're keeping up with the other schools you read about in the papers. This is not a real or effective response to the war machine." There was almost no arguing with them, on this or anything else. They were smart, of course, and they were learned, but above all they were convinced in a way that none of us was—or ever expected to be. We listened; we nodded or murmured very quietly. We asked questions carefully and tentatively, in the age-old student desire not to look the fool.

How much did I learn? Little that lasted about Marx or capital; something about the intellectual history of Marxism; much about the contrasting temperaments and methods of Marx and Engels. Next to nothing about economics, socialist or not. Perhaps more than anything, I learned from these advocates about the workings of a zealous, intelligent, fanatical faith: Hhow it sharpened their analysis of our political situation and made them clear and alert about the hypocrisies and uncertainties afflicting the rest of us in almost everything we did. The more we tried to do the right thing, the idealistic thing (as we would have called it), the more we were befuddled and embarrassed by their harsh critique.

Why did they teach this course? It was a job, I suppose, and a chance to reread and study works of great importance to them. But why did they bring such intensity to their arguments and expositions? It would be much too simple to say that they sought to convert us all to a hard-line Maoism.

They were savvy people, alert and subtle. They knew our tentativeness was not wholly deferential and submissive. They could tell from the start that many of us went along with them, with their course, with a deep reserve of skepticism. And these thick ponderous books of Marx's, while great and powerful, were also flawed and unpolished, crude and imperfect.

I don't know anyone who left the course with a resolve to follow our professors into the Progressive Labor Party, a group whose later evolutions must have troubled even the firm faith of these two teachers.

Yet when I think about how the two advocates took up teaching as a profession, I have to believe that they did it as revolutionaries, as teachers intent on convincing others of the need for and proper direction of a revolution against the social order.

Now there is a view abroad among teachers and scholars that what the advocates did was wrong: they set out to teach the truth in morality and politics, feeling themselves in possession of that truth. They themselves did not much use words like "truth" and "morality." The clash of ideas, of ideologies, was to them a brute fact of all argument and culture. The better idea was the accurate one, the one more exactly predicting the working out of history's logic and end. What is wrong with what they did, some would charge, is that they taught without detachment or openness, with answers rather than questions, with open scorn for those who differed from them.

How should teachers teach? Are they—or should they be—moral teachers as well as chemists, sociologists, or what have you? Or should they simply somehow explore with students, showing the way, raising questions, posing dilemmas, providing information? This is a much more difficult question than it may at first appear.

When I first started teaching, I was a law professor. I had many illusions about what it would be like. It was the late '70s, and law schools were hiring several new professors every year. A lot of us had very little experience, of teaching or law, and we talked intently about what we were up to. Among the most vivid of those conversations are those that took as a rough theme the question. What can one hope to accomplish by teaching, day-to-day and over a working lifetime? The most exciting and simplest answer that

I recall was the one that went like this: I went into law in order to change this society for the better. I'm going into teaching in the same spirit. For me, the best thing I can do is to radicalize my students so that they too will graduate with a commitment to changing things for the better.

But this account never seemed to me to capture the experience of teaching. It is much too neat for the results that most of us achieve—and strive for.

I taught constitutional law for a dozen years or so. I love the subject—and believe in it. But I learned quickly that I had no stomach for whole classes of students who would see constitutional issues as I did. In fact, it was much more thrilling—and revealing, analytically at least—to have students who took up ideas long since out of fashion or discredited by people like me and the judges and lawyers I admired. The class learned more, it seemed to me, when real differences enlivened the cases and made old principles and old debates vital and even urgent.

A joy and a curse in teaching constitutional law is the almost constant relevance of the subject to what's in the papers and on the evening news. No old case lacks a vivid modern illustration—often one that offers the spectacle of sharp controversy or, at a minimum, sharp irony. But this relevance sometimes curses study and discussion with shallow gestures of opinion-mongering on the part of students or even professors: Marbury and Madison had to be decided the way it was, a student might say, because otherwise the Congress would have no check on its present proclivities to yield all to lobbyists and contributors. One is caught at times like that doing what Mark Edmundson calls rebounding: dignifying a shallow and naive comment with a resonant "yes" that suggests that with a little elaboration and extension such a comment may be seen to raise profound questions. But better than easy relevance the real wonder that stops most of us in our tracks when we encounter something truly strange and hard to understand: Othello's rage, for instance, or the disappearance of Neanderthals, or the amazing simplicity of the earthworm called *C. elegans*. Yes, connections to the everyday and the contemporary are helpful and enjoyable; but much does not connect easily or lightly or quickly.

Complacency is a moral category, along with many others, and I found—

as most teachers and students do—that the facile analogy or discussion, even the agreeably interested one, did not hold for me or my students much that was bracing or challenging or revealing.

No teacher is so graced as to have student dissenters ready and willing in every class. I found that the classes I taught were worst when all agreed, often blandly, on the received opinions or common wisdoms of constitutional law. So much was this true that no cases were harder to teach than those where bedrock moral principles were declared in ways that seemed to me and my students self-evident. As the semesters went on, I found myself dissenting, awkwardly at first, feeling sometimes dishonest or disingenuous, but then with increasing conviction. I kept coming back to the feeling that I was there, as Kierkegaard said, to complicate things, to make them difficult and awkward; to challenge my students—and myself—whenever complacency and easy assent reared themselves up and threatened to dominate an hour's discussion.

In effect, I found myself inviting, and then prodding, my students to be difficult, intellectually difficult, to resist the easy or obvious path, even when I felt sure that it was the morally or politically righteous one. One professor tells his students to be Kramers and not Seinfelds. Be crazy rather than cool, wild rather than tame, odd rather than ordinary.

There are many ways to challenge one's own and one's students' assumptions, but I will call this style of teaching the teacher as devil's advocate. I want to make the contrast plain between the advocates who taught what they themselves believed in, passionately, and the devil's advocates among us, who try to teach against either what they themselves believe or else against what they suspect their students will all too likely believe.

For me, there are two surprises in this comparison of teaching styles. The first is this: I find that I cannot really take sides between the two. Both seem to me important to the liveliness and rigor of a curriculum. Something in me prefers the advocate to the devil's advocate, I admit. It may be the frankness and directness of the approach. It may be simply that as I remember my own teachers, it is the oddballs, the true believers, the zealots who stand out. But it goes against my own practice as a teacher and that of most of my colleagues. Most of us see ourselves not as purveyors of views but as challengers of assumptions. The second thing that surprises me in the comparison is how both approaches seem to merge when we think hard about the actual practices and purposes of teachers.

Real advocates and devil's advocates alike do not want to build in straw. Solid foundations matter more than anything else to people with a passion for ideas. The most zealous true believer, setting out to convert her students, does not want them to come round too easily. "I would not lead you into the promised land if I could," said Eugene Victor Debs to his followers, "because if I could lead you in, someone else could lead you out." My two instructors in the work of the mature Karl Marx didn't want us to buy in so much as they wanted us to listen and possibly heed a powerful critique of our own society and *its* foundations. They were believers, yes, but they didn't just want us to fall in with their beliefs. As they saw it, they had worked at them, examined alternatives, tested concepts and assumptions against study and experience.

I have had many great teachers, but few of the great ones were people with whom I agreed in the obvious points of politics or morality. The great ones inspired me with their passion for the truth and, above all, their passion to reexamine and to question. And this was true, it seems to me, wherever they fell across the spectrum from true believer to skeptic or even cynic.

None of us ever fully eludes true belief, or dogmatism. Bits of it cling to us in one way or another, like thistles in wool socks. Some make their dogmas obvious in the grand scale with which they dissent from ideas to which most of us nod. It is easy to see the dogmatism in the Maoist or the mystic, the positivist or the Platonist. What's harder to catch is the dogma in skepticism, the rhetoric in doubt. Assumptions are as necessary to intellectual life as hypotheses and questions. The purpose of the great teacher, the hidden purpose, is to get at the assumptions—and to test them: to see how they work, where they come from, what they imply. And always the great teacher asks, "What *other* assumptions might we make here?"

Is this a moral purpose? Is there a morality in this characteristic way of teaching? There is, but it is not the morality that critics of colleges and universities sometimes call for, the unambiguous morality of "do this" and "don't do that." We, too, require definiteness at times at college, and thus proscribe wrongdoing in the residential halls—assault or theft, say—and in the classroom, as well. We have an absolute prohibition on plagiarism, on submitting another's work as one's own. But the real morality we teach is the morality of freedom, of free inquiry and free conviction.

It begins with an assumption, an act of faith: you the students have the intelligence and maturity to think for yourselves, to make up your own minds and to respond to challenges—from us, from your classmates, from within yourselves.

As I look back now on the most passionately committed of my teachers—a mystic, an existentialist, an anthropologist, a constitutional lawyer—all of them went before their students with this faith. Whatever else they believed in, they believed in their students' ability to respond to serious challenge. They had no sense that we could not take it, that we would need coddling or soft-pedaling. This is not to say that they had no patience for learning, for the time it took us to acquire the rudiments of a discipline and some of its background information.

But there was urgency in their teaching. You will see it in your own teachers, when they push harder than you would like or dismiss a plausible answer as inadequate. The urgency is there because the stakes are high. What hangs in the balance is not the question that will often worry you in class and in exams: am I smart enough, can I keep up with or even outdo my peers?

The bigger, more enduring question, the one you will have to ask yourself as long as you live is this: Are my thoughts and stances my own? Do I deserve the respect of these teachers, deserve it because I am what they deeply want me to be—not a clone of theirs or a convert but a free, independent thinker, an adult with the courage and tenacity to come to my own convictions?

To say that the mind is free is in some ways a paradox. Immanuel Kant demonstrated how difficult it is to believe in freedom by showing the inescapability of determinism—of unfreedom—and yet its moral impossibility. He called his demonstration an antinomy, or contradiction. For most of us, moral life is full of contradictory principles. But Kant was right to make freedom the basis of the moral life. In this, and in his faith in human reason, he is perhaps the greatest philosopher of the liberal arts.

Kant's most powerful image was of human moral life as a kingdom of ends, not means, a kingdom in which we treat one another, as he put it, as ends in ourselves, as deserving the respect that a moral being deserves for its freedom and its rationality. It is an apt image for us. A college ought to be a kingdom of ends, where each of us thinks and chooses unhindered by convention and conformity and where we treat one another as equally capable of freedom and rationality. This is an ideal; we sometimes fall short of it. But I urge it on you as a worthy ideal for a community of students and scholars.

Heraclitus on Campus

I wrote my senior thesis on Heraclitus of Ephesus. I knew nothing of him when I went to college. But over senior year, like many of you, I labored away over obscure references and far-fetched interpretations, trying to make sense of a hundred or more scattered words and phrases of ancient Greek set down on the coast of Turkey 2,500 years ago. Why him? You might ask, as sometimes still I ask myself. I will try to answer that question, as a way of asking why any of us study and what our choices add up to.

When I was in high school, I read Simone Weil's great essay on the *Iliad*, "the poem," as she called it, "of violence." In it, and in her other writings, she often gave Greek citations in the original. I liked the way the letters looked, with more squiggles and accents than the letters in English or Latin or French. When I first got to college, I took ancient Greek philosophy and loved the earliest of these philosophers who wrote so little and had such magnificent names: Anaxagoras, who said that mind or intelligence controls all things; and Parmenides, who thought that appearances and sensations mask a vast unity of being hidden behind what we see and feel. I think the first thing I read of Heraclitus was the fragment that says that dry souls are best.

I found it striking and exciting: primitive, I suppose, but powerful and suggestive. Souls, he thought, are made of fire. To me, this meant that the best portions of our identities are fiery in the metaphorical sense: full of heat and light and possibly rebellion.

He wrote in a distant language and place, using words that we translate only approximately. We have talked of souls for hundreds of years in religious traditions undreamt of by Heraclitus. Fire is still fire, I suppose, but many of its uses—and perhaps much of its mystery—may have disappeared for us. Even if we can learn his language, its vocabulary and syntax, we can never be sure that we will ever understand just what he meant by much of what he said.

All of Heraclitus' writings are called "fragments" because we find them in broken clauses and phrases in the works of later Greek philosophers and historians. The words attributed to him show up as shards or remnants in the reports of his life and ideas. And given the distance that separated him from these later writers, we can be reasonably sure that what they say about him is inaccurate.

We have little idea how Heraclitus lived or died. He was from Ephesus; his name and education bespeak privilege; his words tell us all we will ever know of his life.

I was drawn to the obscurity of Heraclitus, as well as to the fragments themselves. This was a philosopher about whom *no one* knew much. The apprentice scholar had as good a shot at him as the most venerable professor. Many students pick paper topics or majors in a similar spirit of exploration, with a sense that you might be the first person to understand a Russian poem or a rock formation or the economics of prejudice.

None of us is immune to the dream of Columbus, much as we know that there never was a Columbus in this sense: a first human on far-off shores, a discoverer whom no one preceded. Columbus was not even the first from his own continent, but simply, accidentally, the first in the complicated and tragi-comic line that leads us to where we are here and now. In learning, no one is a Columbus. Yes, there are discoveries—in archeological digs, in literary texts, in chemistry and physics and sports. But mostly we go where others have gone before us, noticing, if we are lucky, something they missed or perhaps misunderstood.

All along the path, we can notice where others have either preceded us or else pointed the way.

But Heraclitus was doubly obscure: not just unknown and almost unknowable, but also paradoxical and willfully difficult. There is good reason for his reputation, in literary traditions, for a kind of snarling reclusiveness. It is his words and sentences that snarl at us and go into hiding. Heraclitus said such things as "The road up and the road down are the same road" and "You cannot step twice into the same river." In a famous fragment, he is said to have commented, about a fire in a hearth, "there are gods in there, too." What exactly he meant by this will be forever uncertain. He may have meant to shock those who thought the gods were in the temples or on Olympus. He may have meant to suggest that all fire is divine, like the fire in the sun. He may have meant to say that the names people gave to the gods only concealed the truth that the divine is present in the everyday.

But knowing that Heraclitus was hard to understand only made the attempt more alluring. Yeats speaks of "the fascination of what's difficult." In literary archeology such as this, there is uncertainty but also great freedom to imagine and conjure. No one can prove you wrong, though neither can you prove yourself right.

Some of you will have studied as I did, hard and freely, with joy in the play of such material. Others of you will have been more disciplined in your taste and more rigorous in your results. No matter; I take Heraclitus as my ancient guide to what you—what we all—have been about. All knowledge courts certainty amid obscurity. All of it risks refutation and revision. None of it stands still for long.

Heraclitus believed that reason, what he called *Logos,* was everywhere and in all things, much as we often fail to grasp it. Repeatedly he said that we are asleep to what goes on before us and around us. "Nature loves to hide" was one of his most noted sayings. We go through life like sleepwalkers, he thought, bumping into this and that obstacle We imagine it to be something familiar or something frightful, but too rarely examining it or inquiring how it functions and why. Our task, our intellectual task, is simply to wake up.

If there is a faith underlying our studies, all of them together, it is a faith in questions, in inquiry. Our answers comfort for a time, but most of them are provisional and incomplete. Learning is hard; and more than hard, it is unending. Yet most of us persist in believing that we can make headway, that we can learn something more than initial impressions or judgments tell us: that we can learn, at a minimum, which questions get us nowhere, and which seem hopeful and of lasting interest. Probably the most radical witness to that faith is the insistence by your professors that even as a brand-new student you could indeed take on the hardest questions of philosophy or painting or anthropology. They press you in these four years, as Heraclitus pressed those who listened to him. "If you do not hope for the *un*hoped for," he said, "you will not discover it, since it is undiscovered and no paths lead there."

When I set out to study Heraclitus, I felt the romance of inquiry as well as its faith. Here was something distant from me, odd, known to few people, and difficult. It required another language, an ancient one, with all the uncertainties that go with a language that no one speaks. Moreover, Heraclitus challenged us, as great teachers can, with paradoxes and riddles.

I loved to study the words themselves: to look at them in Greek, just as Diogenes and Aristotle must have. Research has this tactile joy for most of us: chalk and a blackboard for the mathematician; vials and the steel hood for the chemist; library stacks and the old manuscripts for the critic or historian.

Above all, I was drawn to the *ideas* in these words. That's what it means to be a student or an intellectual, you may say. Yes it is, but to be drawn, as if by nature, toward generalizations, speculations, imagery of all kinds, is also a portion of what it means to be human.

The main ideas of Heraclitus are few, if surprisingly striking and forceful.

HERACLITUS ON CAMPUS

Throughout his fragments, there is an emphasis on a unity concealed by disunity or opposition. In one of his most beautiful images, Heraclitus invokes divinity: "God is day and night, winter and summer, war and peace, fullness and hunger, changing as fire does when spices are thrown in and it takes the name of each."

I offer you then three Heraclitean ideas: first, the idea that there is a *Logos* or reason to all things, undiscovered as it may be. This seems to me to be the faith of all of us in every field of inquiry. It is intrinsic to the sciences and social sciences. It is implicit in history and biography, painting and theater, as we try, again and again, to understand what at first baffles us.

Second, Heraclitus believed that change is a constant of, and essential to, this order or reason that we can find by dint of inquiry. He put this law of change most vividly and concretely in a fragment that says that even "the sun is new each day." Like the river it has much less fixity than we think. Those of us who study the classics have sometimes prided ourselves on the apparent fixity of the writers and philosophers of ancient Rome and Greece. But the lesson of our own lifetimes is radically different: Plato, the Parthenon, the Greek or Roman family—all have changed as we have changed and our approaches and inquiries have changed. Those who believe in fixity in curriculum, in work, even in nature—they call out, like the Nordic king, who wanted to stop the tide against ideas more powerful than we know.

What follows from this is a third aspect of Heraclitus' philosophy, the insistence that clashes, oppositions, and struggles are implicit in all existence, in all changes. "We must know," he said, "that war is universal and justice is struggle and that all things come to be in strife and necessity." This is not to say, with Hobbes, that we live a war "of all against all." "People do not recognize," Heraclitus said, "that disagreeing is itself agreement." He used a striking image for this: the bent wood of a bow pulled taut and tense by a cord, whether to fling arrows or, as in the Greek lyre, to make music. We are pulled taut by argument but the result can be music—or even community.

When you study an organism, or a culture, or a poem, you must feel some of what I felt in studying Heraclitus: the wonder at the intelligence in these peculiar sayings; the puzzlement at what they meant and what held them together; the intrigue at their oddity, their differentness

Many of you have studied things more paradoxical, more remote, and more mysterious than Heraclitus. His Greek is, after all, the language of a civilization naively but learnedly almost worshiped in our own traditions of law and literature. He stands with a handful of other philosophers, including Socrates, Plato, and Aristotle, at one of the first forks in the great European path that was to divide into philosophy, on the one hand, and science, on the other. In literature and in philosophy in our own waning century, Heraclitus is a familiar figure of dissidence and rebellion. We find him cited or echoed in Nietzsche and Heidegger, in Simone Weil, and even in Derrida and Foucault.

I had not traveled far, after all. And this, too, may be a lesson of your studies—and your lives. Just when you think you have gone the farthest from your starting point, you will see, in yourself or in what surrounds you, something surprisingly familiar, something modest, perhaps. Let it keep you from the arrogance of discovery or accomplishment. Yes, you will have come a long way, and learned a great deal; but no life takes us so far, no learning teaches us so much, that we should lose sight of the shore from which we launched.

We talk about a world out there, beyond this campus and beyond these four years, as if it were a different world, a new one, with new rules and new realities. I am never sure whether this is a way of denying something important about the college community—its frustrations, perhaps, or its limits—or of asserting something about the way our lives should unfold when we leave. If, as Heraclitus insists, the differences we cling to are often illusory, then we should take some care with this casual dualism.

There is no field of study or endeavor in which the laws of Heraclitus—the laws of change, of strife, of paradox, do not hold. Whatever you study, I hope you will learn this.

Heraclitus wrote often of the fire in our souls. He once said that "You will not find the limits of the soul, even if you travel down its every path: its *Logos* is too deep." You will not soon find your own limits either, no matter how far you go. But be guided by your sense of self, of your own dry and fiery souls. The most beautiful of Heraclitus' fragments consists of three Greek words: *ethos anthropoi daimon*. Character, for human beings, is fate. May your characters be fiery and sturdy, full of curiosity and compassion. And may *your* fates be kind and lively.

Stealing Painted Bicycles

When I was in my last semester at law school, I went to the registrar for a transcript of my grades and credits. The room had a counter where I waited for help. It was late Friday afternoon, and the woman on duty was all by herself. When I first came in, she was busy with a phone call. When she finished, she asked for my name and some identification; she told me I needed to pay a few dollars for each of the several copies I wanted sent out. I wrote out the names and addresses of those to whom the transcripts were to go, and I wrote a check as she had told me. But by this time she had picked up the phone again. She shrugged at me as if to say, "What can I do?" I waited for her to finish the conversation. While she talked, she pulled out a file drawer and found my transcript, a surprisingly simple printed card. She waved this in the air as she gestured to the person on the other end of the line. The conversation went on, punctuated by an occasional shrug for my sake. I realized this was going to take a while. Then, still talking busily on the phone, she came to the counter and handed me the card, for inspection I assumed. I looked it over and nodded: the grades were familiar, though I was struck by the various pens that had been used and one splotch of whiteout, where one of my law teachers must have changed his mind about my paper or exam. I wondered about that but just looked up at her with a nod that was meant to suggest that "Yeah, this is the right one all right." Instead of taking it back, though, she mouthed the word "copy," pointed to the door and the corridor, and held up five fingers for the number of copies I wanted sent out. I knew there was a copy machine outside because I had used it once before and because someone was often there in the corridor copying one thing or another. I was dumbfounded as I realized that she wanted me to copy my own transcript while she went on talking on the phone. I turned, went out to the machine in the corridor, pushed the number 5, brought back the copies, and waited for her once again. With the phone at her ear, she gave me a little wave of thank you.

Now, I had good grades but, I will admit here, not perfect grades. As I left the building to go home, I felt a wave of relief and astonishment that I had just escaped the temptation to make my law school record absolutely perfect. What astonished me at the time was how trusting she was of my honesty—or was it only that she was so involved in her phone conversation that she never even thought I might change a grade or two out in the corridor?

Life is full of dishonesty. Most of us realize this fleetingly, as we evade a request for a meeting or tell someone that we liked a poem that we found silly or not as funny or clever as they hoped. In schools, as in love, we call the chief form of dishonesty cheating. It is one of those things in the background of our lives as students and teachers, whether as a temptation or a fact. Occasionally a cheater is caught out in a painful incident.

Some time ago, many of us watched in grim fascination as one of the best scholars I knew was shown to have lied to his students repeatedly about his bogu experience of combat during the Vietnam War. Some people tried to defend these classroom lies by saying, glibly, that we all lie at times—which is certainly true. Huck Finn had it that "I never seen anybody but lied one time or another." But the point is that students trust their teachers to tell them what they know—or think they know—to be true. And conversely, we teachers trust you students to tell us truthfully what you know, what you have learned. But if lying is as old as talking and writing, then cheating may well be as old as tests and courses.

In cheating, we not only take ideas from someone else—which almost all intellectuals do and have to do—but we then pass them off as our own, as our own discoveries or insights, as the product of our own work, unaided by others. The "taking" of ideas, the exchanging of ideas, is innocent—innocent, that is, unless we conceal their origins and our debt to others.

In Holland, back in the '70s, free bicycles were distributed around the town for all to use they were painted a bright white so that you couldn't miss them. Taking them was perfectly all right, as long as you left them again for the next person to come along. But the system broke down when people took them and either wrecked them or repainted them in various colors so as to steal them. Intellectual life requires us to use the common bicycles—the insights and ideas put there by others. But we do this on the understanding that we owe each other an honest acknowledgment of where the ideas came from. The system of free bicycles broke down quickly once a few thieves went to work. The system of free ideas is much tougher to wreck. Cheaters have not done nearly so much harm. But they do betray the understanding under which we all work: that we will own up to the sources of our ideas and account for them by saying, "I found this idea here, check it out. I owe this other idea to so-and-so."

When any of us cheat in school—in research, in tests, in discussions—we paint ideas a new color, as if to say, "These are mine . . . I did the work that you see or hear: I get the credit for it." We lie about work in order to steal the credit. And often we can get away with this lie for the simple reason that we trust each other. Academic life, like friendship, requires trust, which is what frees us up to argue hard and with conviction.

Plagiarism is a kind of intellectual theft, like making off with a Dutch bicycle. But the analogy is imperfect, or at least vulnerable to a sharp critique, for its suggestion that knowledge is somehow like money or a possession.

Knowledge is not like money. If I earn $100 and you take it from me, I will have lost it. But if I learn an operation in calculus and you take that from me, I still *have* it—and you never really got it; you never learned it. What you did get was a counterfeit of knowledge that worked for this one purpose, for getting through a course with a passing grade on the exam.

Cheating is sometimes defended in more or less this way. No one loses anything. I take the grade and the credit without doing the work, it is true, but I don't take it *from* anyone. The person whose answer or paper I copy loses nothing. He or she got—or will get—full credit for work done. If it's plagiarism from published work, the author will know nothing about my use of it—and the author's reputation and royalties will hardly be affected by an undergraduate's illicit use of the material. Thus more than one undergraduate plagiarist has responded indignantly when caught by a professor, "What difference do little quotation marks make?" In its own way, this is a profoundly important question for a college, for those of us who teach, and above all for you who study. What difference *does* cheating make to us all?

There is always an element of shock in the discovery of a cheating episode, particularly one that involves several students. But the shock is never evenly distributed: the faculty and its deans are almost always caught by surprise by these incidents. They had thought them rare and improbable among bright and motivated students. The alumni and the board of trustees are usually dismayed. "It makes no sense at all for *our* students," they say. I'm not sure what parents think of such incidents. I mostly hear from the outraged parents—and lawyers—of those who are accused. But the students are almost never so shocked as the rest of us. "I see a fair amount of cheating," one of the editors of the student paper told me. "It's just rare that anyone gets caught."

On most campuses, we see a spike in the number of cases brought before disciplinary committees. College councils—which usually include students, faculty members, and deans—review policies and practices at length and in depth.

There have been many surveys of cheating and academic dishonesty on campuses. None that I have seen can pretend to much certainty. In the early 1970s, an anonymous survey of Amherst College students yielded admissions from more than a third of those who responded that they themselves had cheated at least once. There were some curiosities in the survey questions—and in its results. Sadly, but perhaps predictably, those who felt the most pressure, those with a set of definite prerequisites for graduate school, cheated at a higher rate than others. This suggests that the leading condition in cheating of all kinds is pressure, competition. But the survey didn't define cheating with any precision. Presumably, someone who will cheat on an exam will also lie about it. So it is possible that more students cheat than say they do, even anonymously.

Research suggests a range of frequency of cheating on roughly this order: from 30 to 60 percent of students will acknowledge anonymously that they have cheated at least once in an undergraduate career. Male students seem to cheat more than female students; students sworn to uphold an honor code—with an obligation to report one another—seem to cheat less than others.

The question is, will you be among them? If not, why not? Why does it matter?

You came to college as someone who studied well and studied hard. It is an odd place to come in order to slack off and cheat, even occasionally. But still, it's worth asking why anyone would cheat. Certainly there will be moments of temptation; most students that I talk to about it say that cheating is most common among two kinds of students, the disaffected and the insecure.

If you are frightened of college, frightened that you will fail, then panic may push you to do all sorts of things that will seem stupid in hindsight. Reports give many instances of students saying that they fear they will not live up to expectations—their own, their families', their friends'. This fear, combined with piled-up homework and an especially tough course, may throw a student into a frenzied search for a way to come up with an assured grade.

There is a thick streak of irrationality in this panic: admission offices spent a lot of time selecting each of you in preference to others; their chief criterion—always—is the student's ability to thrive intellectually. A student in the '70s said that the fearful cheater was like the nation's then fearful president, Richard Nixon, who used illegal methods in his campaign for re-election despite overwhelming odds of victory. Like Nixon, the fearful cheater is likely to destroy precisely what he or she wanted to secure by panicky acts of dishonesty.

Conditions for which we bear some responsibility *might* contribute to the temptation to cheat in a panic: first, we as teachers need to make sure that our students know the boundaries between legitimate cooperation, legitimate citation, and plagiarizing from others, whether scholars or peers. Our advice has to be plain: always make clear to us where ideas have come from. The second condition, in which we as an institution have a part, is that we owe it to our students and to ourselves to acknowledge the dangers and temptations of cheating and to guard against them as best we can. For many years, colleges have favored a tradition of no proctors in exams. The professor has every right to come and go, should she or he choose to do so, but typically no one will be there watching while you take an exam. This is an aspect of our understanding that you are adults, on your honor, to be respected as such. It is a notable feature of college and extends to the curriculum and residential life both. You are on your own here; we trust you to make sound choices. But we *can* sometimes trust too much, and thus tempt students into mistakes that all of us will regret.

The third condition is that we teachers stand ready to help. You should know that we do, that that is among our purposes.

Finally, though, I should mention one condition of institutional life over which we have less control than we might imagine. All of us, in all our roles on campus, derive some advantage from the place of the college in the hierarchy not just of American colleges and universities, but also in the larger world of American political, economic, and cultural life. We can hold out loud and long for the intrinsic worth of our studies together, but they are assigned an extrinsic worth as well.

College is a credential, as we say: a curious word, meaning a mark of faith or belief, of credit—something in which others can put their faith, their credence. Credentials were originally diplomatic letters telling one court to accept—and trust—ambassadors from another. Similarly, our credits in courses are marks of a level of achievement. None of us should be so naive as to ignore the dual nature of a college education—something we hold dear for its own qualities of study and insight, but something the world values as a multifarious credential suggesting prestige, connections, perhaps intelligence. The sociologist, Andrew Hacker speaks often of the finishing-school aspect of college.

Because college *is* a credential, one can take something valuable from it even without learning a thing in our courses. And this is perhaps the most abiding temptation to cheat: cheating gets something for free, not learning but the substitute for learning, its credential. Whether we cheat on a single test or a whole course, or on all tests in all courses, the gain is that we get something that others have had to work for, and we get it for free. We become free riders on the college's reputation for turning out well-educated graduates.

Free riding appeals to all of us, I suspect. We are all lazy in one measure or another, and we shouldn't underestimate laziness as a motivation for cheating: we all have the desire, all things considered, to expend as little effort as possible to get what we want.

But I have the impression that simple laziness accounts for less cheating and dishonesty than this implies. Laziness, after all, as Socrates might have said, is itself lazy: its ideal is that we should expend no effort at all. Laziness has to join with the desire to get hold of at least the credential of learning before it would push any of us to take the risks of cheating.

And this leads me back to ideas, which is what college is really about. The few times I've discussed cheating with someone who has both done it and owned up to it, I've been struck not by the laziness of the person but, to the contrary, by the energy of both the enterprise and the explanation. It takes some effort to devise a method for cheating; it takes even more, it seems, to convince ourselves that we were right to do so—or at least not so very wrong. And in this sense the cheater is an old-fashioned philosopher, interested like the rest of us in argument and ideas.

The cheater's main ideas seem to be these: Everyone around us values credentials more than they should. Students compete with one another for good grades so as to get into good graduate schools so as to get good jobs. All of this competition for grades makes a travesty of learning. So the smartest thing to do is to subvert the immoral system and grab what really counts, which turns out to be the grade.

This is a moral and political argument at heart. But at best it is an unconvincing one. If the system *is* immoral, then we ought to get rid of it—and the sooner the better. Fight to abolish grades or, if that's utopian and unrealistic, vow to work for learning only. Cheating for grades only makes things worse: it puts grades before all else, before learning and ideas.

Twenty or thirty years from now, you will recall your first days on campus. You will remember faces and friends, some late-night conversations, a professor's opening lecture. You're not likely to recall what I say or what the deans said during orientation. But I guarantee you that you will remember any cheating that you do or see. No college can save any of us from the temptation. And it would be a lesser place that would try too hard: less free, less trusting, less interested in your ideas and your learning. No college, no law, can guard us safely from dishonesty in our studies or our careers or our personal lives. But I urge you to guard yourselves from betraying so much of what you came here to do.

CITIZENSHIP

Country and City

I grew up in the country, or what seemed to me the country. We had fields all around our house, with woods beyond them. In the spring, Mr. Ference came with his tractor to turn the ground and plant rows of corn and potatoes. All summer we would hide in the cornrows or make our way through them to their mysterious honeysuckled borders, near the stone wall at the edge of the woods. Three giant maples stood astride the fields, perhaps a quarter mile back from our yard.

 To me, the country meant solitude: there was no one to play with except my own brothers. Across the street from us lived Newton Hawkins and his sister, an ancient pair in an ancient house. Because of his name, I will forever associate them with the invention and production of what to me was the most exquisite delicacy of my childhood, the fig newton. They drew their water from a well and had no plumbing. They were reported to be the last of their line; they and their ancestors farmed land that over two centuries had been sold down to less than an acre.

On holidays, we always went to the city. New York City was to me, in those first few years after the Second World War, a splendid if somewhat daunting gathering of people, places, zoos, skyscrapers, museums, and shops. My immigrant grandparents lived there, with hot pretzels and strong brogues and close neighbors.

All my life I have loved cities, loved them as only a child of the country can love them, as a convert, a yearner, a dreamer for whom they live partly in fantasy and ideal. As soon as I could get away from the country, I did: to Paris for the last year of high school, to Lima, Peru, for one year of college, to New Haven and Chicago and Pittsburgh and Cincinnati and to Hartford. Cities have always held out to me the promise—even in their sounds and smells—of adventure, of ideas, of music and art, of markets and conversation.

Few of us can be blessed with the wisdom to know more than a portion of what really goes on around us. Was it Hegel who said that what is familiar is what is hardest to see and understand? For children, time meanders among a few landmarks: the corner store, the playground, the walk or ride to school. Later, time rushes by, or seems to, no longer a rivulet but a river.

Coming back to Connecticut after years away, I had the impression, on Hartford's streets, that little had changed: the three-family houses on Crescent and Broad, the kids in the doorways, the bustle of commuters downtown. This looked to me like New Haven or Bridgeport twenty years before, when I was still a student. But in my lifetime, and in yours, a great shift has taken place in the life of cities.

My father and mother moved to the country to rear a family in green and quiet, near woods and fields. But my father was no country-person; he was a new variety of American: a suburbanite. He commuted by train to the city; all over the United States (and, a little later, over much of Europe) commuters in cars and trains were building houses farther and farther from the great centers of work and culture. Soon the farms began to disappear. Mr. and Mrs. Hawkins died; Mr. Ference no longer baled hay in the heat at the end of summer.

COUNTRY AND CITY

Millions and millions of us have participated in this process of transformation. What one scholar has called the "crabgrass frontier" has lured us on as irresistibly as the Western frontier did in the nineteenth century.

"First, the people went to the suburbs to live," someone said to me. "Then the shops went to the suburbs; and now the jobs are moving to the suburbs."

What I saw as a child was a lush countryside and an equally lush, if very different, city.

What I did not see—and what now we cannot fail to see—is that the America of suburbs leaves neither the countryside nor the cities intact. And plainly, it is the cities that suffer most.

Several days after the 1992 riots in Los Angeles, commentators began to compare what had happened there with the riots of the late 1960s. The photographs showed what had become of neighborhoods and streets in Newark and Detroit and Chicago, burned out and vandalized a long time ago. With few exceptions, they remain now, a quarter-century later, just as they were in the days after their riots. Stores that were burned down often do not reopen; houses rarely go up again in a neighborhood destroyed in a night.

What happened in Los Angeles, in anarchy and anger, is striking and vivid to us now, as it should be. But it should be no more vivid or striking than what we see around us in nearly every city in the nation.

Those who can choose where they will live or work are choosing too often against cities. The result, should we let this go on much longer, will be that our cities will die. In their place will rise up "edge" cities, built up around monotonous successions of malls—for shopping, for work, for schooling, for housing, for entertainment, and, above all, for parking.

What we will lose should America lose its cities is incalculable. Some, like Jane Jacobs, the great champion of street life, believe that without cities a nation can have no economic future. She argues from history: great cities bring together the skills and energy and markets that foster industry and invention.

It is a good argument. Still, it may prove false; perhaps we can have a strong economy without strong cities.

There are even better arguments for saving our cities.

Whatever our economic future, our cultural future without cities is barren and meager. If somehow invention and industry survive without cities, will theaters and museums and symphonies? Cities provide the one ecological niche where human beings push themselves to greater and greater achievements, not only in commerce but in all the arts, especially the highest and most complex.

Patriotism, too, requires of us a standard of national achievement. We cannot lose our pride in our cities without losing some measure of our pride in our nation. To say of this country that it will someday soon have no great cities, nothing to compare to Paris or Budapest, to Delhi or Cairo, is to say that we will have no settlements of cultural and economic stature to stand alongside those of other nations.

Finally, America's cities are the great integrators of our people, of the new immigrant from Laos, Haiti, or Nicaragua, along with the old immigrant from Poland or Italy, Ireland or England. Cities bring us together and teach us new ideas and new possibilities. They teach us to live with one another; they permit us to see close-up what we all share of the human condition, of its virtues, its vices, and its variable genius for everything from baking to poetry.

When I look out on your future, in a time of some uncertainty, I have no fear for you as individuals. You are sturdy, bright, and tenacious. If the world does not at first open its arms to you, it will in time, if you persevere.

But I do fear for America. We seem as a nation to have fallen into cynicism and apathy; drift seems our only response to what ails us. On our urban frontiers we give way to a greater and greater divide between those who can make choices in their lives and those who cannot. In this direction lies an American South Africa, separated out into camps: to one side the prosperous and choosing; to the other, those for whom there is no chance of prosperity and little to choose from. Our cities in this bleak vision will be the Sowetos of our South Africa: segregated, impoverished, disordered—and without much hope.

This need not happen; we have it in our power to stop it, you and I. *We can call America to its senses and restore its pride in* all *its settlements.*

I charge you, then, with the care of our cities and of their citizens. Athens, said Thucydides, was the teacher of Greece. Our cities, too, teach the glory and promise of America. In forsaking them we forsake the hope of our democracy.

Mental Fight

A college is an argumentative place. People on campus argue over many issues, sometimes issues that the outside world would not understand or think worthy of argument. Principles are articulated for nearly everything that we do. And at times it seems that we do nothing—even eat, drink, or sleep—without first battling over the theory of it, the justice of it. This is right and good, as I see it, and makes a college what it is.

William Blake called it "mental fight," and in his boldest assertion of its rightness said, "I will not cease from mental fight, nor shall my sword sleep in my hand, till we have built Jerusalem in England's green and pleasant land." So too at college there is an unceasing mental fight over what it means to have this college on this hill built and rebuilt daily by students, by faculty, by staff, by alumni.

I want to urge you to keep on fighting, to keep on arguing, in the tradition of the campus and its scholars. Think of it as a place where everything is challenged, yes; but think of it too as a place where some things are put forward and defended with the sword of argument. These two intellectual postures—of question and assertion—will prove vital to your intellectual and moral lives in the years to come. Works of the imagination, works of reason, works of compassion: all must take some question as their own and make some assertion, some statement of faith, in response to the world.

More mental fight is needed precisely because mental fight substitutes for and makes unnecessary the physical fight that so often settles questions in the world at large. "Rouse up," Blake said, to stop those who would "forever depress mental and prolong corporeal war."

There can be no Jerusalem, no realized ideal, without sustained mental fight.

Let me give two examples where the American Jerusalem—by which I understand the American democracy—needs more—and more passionate—mental fight.

For many, many years, many colleges have held fast to an ideal of financial assistance that we have described with the awkward term "need blind." It means that we admit our classes without regard to the means of their families to send them here. We say, in effect, "Come to college regardless of your wealth or poverty: if you cannot afford our charges we will reduce them with financial aid." It means as well that we will provide enough aid to make it practical to come. We will, in other words as we say, meet the "full need" of those we invite to come.

We have worried, in the last several years, that our calculations are not generous enough for students with family incomes in the middle range. We have known all along that "generosity" here must be defined in relation both to what families have to spend and to what we can reasonably budget. But "generosity" must also be measured in a marketplace that has become newly frenzied. More and more schools have decided that they will not treat all students equally in distributing financial aid: some will get more than others, not because their families need more help, but because someone has decided that the students in question are more desirable or more deserving than other members of the incoming class. Thus these scholarships are called across the land "merit scholarships"; they go to students without regard to need. They are, in fact, enticement scholarships, meant to promote the enrollment of students with somewhat better grades or SATs or a better passing arm and what have you. So many of our brethren institutions offer these that I hesitate to condemn merit scholarships out of hand.

But as citizens we need to argue this question out with care. If there is a limited amount of money in a college endowment or a government program of financial aid, then it is simple arithmetic to conclude that the more money that goes to those who do not need it, the less there will be for those who do. And as competitive anxieties spread the practice from one institution to the next, then the total amount of money available to those with the greatest need will diminish as the money is used to enroll those deemed meritorious.

We know that we will be pressed to be more generous; I want to hope with you that we will never be pressed so hard as to give up our commitments to an egalitarian admissions process, where financial aid goes to those who most need it. Across the country, and in the Congress in particular, this argument is going to grow more and more heated in the years ahead. And I don't tell you where to stand. But I do tell you to engage in this fight, civilly, thoughtfully, intelligently, but with the passion that comes from a sense of just how much is at stake for our American democracy.

A fierce but none too mental fight now rages in the United States about the next steps beyond civil rights toward real integration—real wholeness—in our democracy.

We all know that the recognition of civil rights for all citizens has not brought us into our American Jerusalem. We still have castes of a sort in America: whole groups of people whose economic and political future is settled almost in advance by their racial or ethnic identities. And the plight of these castes has not much improved—and in some cases has much worsened—in the great internationalization and expansion of our economy over the last decade and more.

Where do we go as a country from here? This is a large question, with many sorts of answers. We on campus have been resolute about one aspect of this question: for a generation and more now, we have believed passionately, on boards, in faculties, among students and alumni, that college classes should be as fully integrated as we can make them. We have practiced an aggressive affirmative action of seeking out qualified students who might not think of this college at first. And we have been definite about the need to have classes where the backgrounds and colors and convictions of our students bespeak an American intellectual leadership truly, if imperfectly, integrated.

There are sharp disagreements in America and in the world about how to reach our Jerusalem of an integrated democracy without castes or exclusions. Some argue that race neutrality or color blindness is what is needed. This is a powerful argument, but not, in my view, a deeply historical or practical one. It is an argument with a question behind it, an urgent question for you in your lives, as for the college in its life: how can we reach the place we all know to be the right place, the place where you can open any door in America, in any office or studio or classroom, and find a person there who found her or his way without race dictating the outcome?

We are committed to the widest possible diversity. We need to take risks as an institution to achieve that diversity. We need to use our resources aggressively, and, above all, to push ourselves hard to approach our ideal of an American Jerusalem. You may disagree with our commitments and policies; we welcome argument, and we welcome disagreement. But I ask you to take on the mental fight needed to keep these questions and commitments before us and our country. A college without diversity is a less interesting, less exciting, less intellectually and morally challenging place. It is not the campus we know and love, and the one we care enough to fight over. But an America that does not realize its ideals of integration and participation is much worse than uninteresting or unintellectual: it is illegitimate and, in an important sense, undemocratic.

I hope we have challenged you here, each of you. And I hope that you have acquired a taste for mental fight. Go now and challenge yourselves on a wider front and in bigger struggles. Challenge us all and build your own Jerusalem.

Addictions and Hypocrisies

In the summer of 1969, someone gave me and my girlfriend a brownie baked with marijuana. It had an extravagant effect on both of us. I thought a small fire in a woodstove was as large and fearsome (and thrilling!) as hell itself. I later married the girlfriend, my wife, Adelia, but neither of us was ever interested in experimenting further with drugs. Nowadays my sons tell me that I'm such a lightweight that even nonalcoholic beer affects me strangely, and I almost never drink more alcohol than is contained in a single beer or a glass of wine. Still, I want to talk to you about intoxication and addiction.

Clearly, I'm no expert. What strikes me most about our national policy on drugs and alcohol is its hypocrisy. It is an organized and extensive hypocrisy, and one that seems to me silly in the small world of the campus. But it is anything but silly or laughable in the bigger world, where it is observed and promoted with zeal, money—and too often with lives.

Human life is full of hypocrisy, I know. We tell people how much joy or sorrow we feel with them, when we may well feel much more or much less or neither. We are polite to one another, nice to one another, when we would like to scream. We pretend to be and feel many things that we are not. All this helps smooth the rough patches in our shared lives. It spares hurt and bother and allows us to go on to other things. Hypocrisy serves us well much of the time, but not always.

Let me begin with the campus. Over the last twenty years or so, the federal government has used a variety of incentives to promote twenty one as the age of permitted drinking of alcohol. Highway funding, in particular, has long depended on state conformity to this federal policy. Gradually the states have fallen into line, prohibiting those under twenty one from even tasting wine or beer or whiskey. Many states cooperated eagerly in this effort, an effort urged as a remedy, among other things, for drunken driving by teenagers. In this important regard, the policy has contributed to the improvements in driving safety of your generation.

In addition, the Congress has found it satisfying to insist at various points on the evils of what is euphemistically called "substance abuse." Colleges, nearly all colleges, have agreed to report annually on efforts to discourage the use of illegal substances, including alcohol, by those of you not yet twenty one. Should we fail to do these things, and to certify that we do them, we would jeopardize federal financial aid for you and research funds for a number of scientists.

The legislated ideology in these matters is simple and simply stated: these illegal substances are evil, and we should teach you to avoid them all. The only qualification is for alcohol, which is evil until you are twenty one, and then perhaps not evil, or at least not so evil as to be illegal. But for those of you under twenty one, these things are all bad and to be avoided at all times and in all circumstances.

The ideas behind all this may well be complex and nuanced, but they have been simplified, radically simplified, for purposes not only of legislation and enforcement but of official propaganda. These things are evil; teach the

ADDICTIONS AND HYPOCRISIES

young to avoid them. Say no to them, all of them, at all times. There are striking hypocrisies in all this, as there often are in Puritanism. But the colleges are not deeply implicated in these hypocrisies. We shrug and go along with the federal requirements as a formality. It is the *awkwardness* that is most striking for a college dedicated to questioning and probing. On the one hand, we tell you that we have gathered you here with a faculty of scholars and artists to challenge what you may have assumed or been told. On the other hand, we subscribe, in our official capacity, to this simplified approach to what is a universal feature of human cultures—the use of inebriants or intoxicants, often addictive ones, by young and old alike.

Over the years, voters in some towns and cities have made small gestures of protest by passing special ballots to remove the criminal penalties attached to the use of marijuana. But of course these towns have no such authority, and so the vote joins others to hold out against nuclear power or against trade with foreign tyrants.

You who are first-year students will find on campus what you may have found at home: the law frowns on the use of alcohol and the softer illegal drugs, the law threatens and occasionally imposes punishment, but mostly the law lets you do as you would. And the college itself? My job is to speak for the college, and I will try to speak honestly. We cannot, without resort to a kind of local totalitarianism, enforce the prohibition that the government enjoins. Thus we leave you, for the most part, in liberty. I will say, for the college and for myself, that all of these substances can be dangerous to you and your friends. They cause something like half of the fatal car accidents in this nation; they enter into much of the violence between friends and lovers; they are powerful and can grab hold of you and never let go. We cannot easily stop you if you would use them or try them—and so we call out to you, perhaps too often, take care, be wary, exercise caution. If we catch you trading them we will turn you over to the local police. If we catch you in possession of the truly most dangerous drugs we will do the same, asking you to leave campus more or less on the spot.

I mentioned hypocrisy. Are we hypocrites? Not by choice, I can say. We resist the hypocrisy of the government's campaign for clarity and simplicity, for absolute interdiction or denial. We don't preach prohibition, but moderation and caution. But the most critical or cynical amongst you will pick out the inconsistencies and the evasions. We have campus police, some parents say, why not set them to work searching and seizing the contraband substances? We take away kegs when there is no authorization, students complain, so why not go the extra steps and find the beer and the vodka and the marijuana that many of our students use?

One answer is that this residential campus is lax and permissive. Another way to put this is that it is free. The premise under which you enroll here is one of freedom, personal as well as intellectual. Our curriculum has requirements, but they are few. Our residential arrangements require civility and tolerance, but not much more. We give you choices because we believe that you can make them responsibly. Sooner or later you will have to make life choices on your own. This is what we understand by a free society. We say that sooner is better.

I said earlier that our policies involve not just rules, but lives. A petty hypocrisy on campus becomes a tragic one when pursued among those lacking our privileges. The very things that seem silly or stupid on a campus—"Just say no," "Don't even try marijuana," "Wait until you're twenty one to taste a beer"—these have taken on a much more powerful and tragic stupidity in our democracy. Whereas on campus, the hypocrisy is a kind of petty fib, in our society it is much more than that. Hundreds of thousands if not millions of lives are caught up in the maw of our prohibition of drug use, a prohibition probably even less effective off campus than it is on.

Let me give you an instance of the tragic escalation in the cost of these policies as we move from the campus to the society at large.

On campus, race plays almost no part in the incidence of abuse—whether of drugs or alcohol—and no measurable part in the incidence of punishment for offenses under these laws. Our local statistics show, if anything, more usage, more dealing and more punishment among white students than among others. The consequence of this may go unnoticed, but it is important: in a campus setting where discrimination remains a powerfully hurtful and often explosive issue, drug and alcohol abuses seem, if anything, race-blind or race-neutral. This presents an almost absurd contrast to the realities in the world at large.

We know that the abuse of drugs and alcohol has a kind of equal opportunity prevalence in this and other societies. Yes, there are differences across racial and ethnic categories, but no category or grouping is immune. And illegal drugs, in particular, are used throughout American society. But look for a moment at the incidence of punishment in the United States: sifting through various reports on imprisonment, I learn that nearly one quarter of the two million Americans now in prison are serving time for nonviolent drug offenses such as cultivation, sale, and transport. That is nearly half a million people, mostly men, two thirds of them black and Latino men.

State prisons, which vary enormously with the laws and practices of each state, hold most of these offenders, perhaps a quarter of the total prison population. But in the federal prison system more than half of those held have been convicted of nonviolent crimes, such as smuggling and selling drugs. Most of these people are small-time crooks caught up in a worldwide black market in which the American appetite—your appetite—for experimentation and addiction is the great engine.

We cannot know for sure how many of our neighbors use illegal drugs, what drugs they use or in what quantities. But nothing that I read denies the evenhanded racial distribution of usage. Arrest and imprisonment are anything but evenhanded. Black people are as much as fifteen times more likely than whites to be arrested for cocaine usage. The sentences they suffer are hugely disproportionate as well. The one relevant variable between races is that crack has been the form of cocaine most popular in the inner city. Some argue that crack cocaine is more powerful and destructive than cocaine in powder. This may well be true, but does it justify years and years of additional prison time for what is essentially the same crime? And while cocaine is the most extreme example of differential treatment, the racial disproportion remains in every category of illegal usage and dealing.

There are records by which to measure arrest and imprisonment. There is no way to measure with accuracy the contribution of our war on drugs to the violence of our society, and of the world at large. This is an aspect of our policies that has only the faintest shadow on campus. Yes, we experience our share of personal violence on campus: we have rape and sexual assault and, occasionally, an assault with fists. Neither guns nor knives appear on our campus crime logs from one end of the decade to another. The abuse of alcohol, in particular, feeds the violence we experience much as it feeds the violence of our society and most others. But there is no black market in beer and vodka, and there is no gang warfare over the sales territories of their purveyors.

But illegal drugs are different, people will say: they are addictive and dangerous and there is no hypocrisy in saying so—or in making laws that say so. The president of Colombia made headlines saying that narcotrafficking will not end until America curbs its appetite for drugs. Perhaps he is right; perhaps with more effort we will curb or end our national appetite for intoxication. Certainly we will not end it by endlessly arresting and harassing the poor who trade in this for want of anything better. I myself am a skeptic when it comes to any method of ending this very human weakness. Each of us can end it or help end it in ourselves and our loved ones. Some of us can help students or others to end it, or never to indulge in it.

I cannot speak here for anyone but myself. Certainly I cannot speak for any college or any governing board. But speaking for myself, I will say this much: our tradition of study prizes the harsh questioning of the assumptions that we and others make so casually. Hypocrisy and pretense are favorite targets of the critical mind. Sometimes they make easy targets, and we go after them as if to prove our superiority or cleverness. But I do not think this is what is at stake in an attack on the hypocrisies of the drug war. Our intellectual and political tradition rests in the end on the defense of liberty. Self-intoxication is a fundamental question of liberty. To end drug and alcohol abuse on campus would require us to police your lives as if you were children—or convicts. To end this abuse in our society would require an almost inconceivable level of repression. Questions of addiction and dependence are a constant in

ADDICTIONS AND HYPOCRISIES

human life, and no society has altogether banished them. The human body and the human mind surrender all too easily to the illness of addiction, and the materials for it are never far from hand. The temptation will always be present, for all of us.

You in your lives will have to wrestle over and again with questions of your own dependence on substances that may quickly or slowly destroy your will or your body. For some of you, it will be marijuana or tobacco. For many, it will be alcohol. For some, it will be a synthetic drug that makes its way into fashion. Addiction is a surrender of the will, a surrender of liberty. In small ways, nearly every day, we struggle to establish and reestablish a hold over appetites that can pull us toward an abyss.

For me, as a husband and father, as a man, these are among the most important moral questions we face. And we face them on our own. The law can steer us a little, I know; the law can prod us toward what our legislators think to be—or pretend to be—the right balance. But no law and no legislator can save any of us from a will bent toward addiction, whatever the legality or illegality of what tempts us.

Socrates Citizen

Years ago, when I was in high school in France, I read some Plato and came under the spell of Socrates. I count it as my beginning in the liberal arts. We know there is no endpoint to inquiry or discussion, but there are markers along the way. You pass one today, and so do I. I return to Socrates as you and I finish up our work together.

When I first read Socrates' words, they were translated into French. I was living alone in Paris, a yearning adolescent, full of rebellion and solitude. Late nights I would sit at my desk with a cup of watery hot chocolate in front of my book. I remember still the curlicue look of the Greek words for *soul* and *virtue* dangling at the bottom of the French page. What made Socrates so captivating for me was the constant play, in his life and words, between a passionate idealism and the insistent irony with which he challenged himself and others to think harder and more skeptically.

In Plato's *Apology*, Socrates gave what may be the most eloquent legal defense ever recorded. He began by saying how poor and bumbling a speaker he was. "My accusers say I am a gifted, fearsome, speaker," he said. "The only clever thing I have to speak is the truth."[1]

He tells the jurors how surprised he was to learn that the Oracle of Delphi, the local soothsayer, was saying that no man was wiser than Socrates. "How can this be?" he asks, in what seems to us completely feigned astonishment. But I suspect that he was astonished. He took the Oracle's word as a kind of mission: why in the world would anyone think Socrates wiser than others? He questioned all those who were known for their knowledge, their wisdom. What he found was that they knew less than they claimed to know. That, in turn, led to the famous, irksome insight, that "I am wise because I know that I do not know." And the corollary to this, proven again and again in his conversations with the great and glorious, was that wise men everywhere were fools to think they knew much at all about what really mattered—"the care," as he said, "of the soul."

At his trial, Socrates was condemned on two well-documented charges. Plato tells us in the *Apology* that the charges included impiety—not believing in the ruling mythology or theology of Athens—and corrupting the young, presumably by teaching them to question their elders, sometimes with the exasperating obsessiveness and skepticism that I found so alluring at seventeen. In addition to these charges, there were other, unstated charges against Socrates—prejudices, really—against his friendships, his questions, his whole way of living and thinking, of philosophizing, in the small world that was classical Athens. Thus Socrates has to insist that he was never one of the natural philosophers whom Aristophanes and others mocked. Socrates says over and again that he had only one concern, the care of the soul. Today we would call him a moral philosopher.

One of the most powerful of the tacit or hidden charges against Socrates was that he had remained aloof from the rest of Athens' citizens. He was disengaged—detached—from the civic obligations of his nation-state.

---

1. I translate the various passages of Socrates' defense from the Loeb edition of Plato's *Apology*.

He had a good, patriotic defense against this charge: he had been a brave soldier, holding his ground more than once as an infantryman abroad in Athens' wars; what's more, he had been a brave citizen at home, once resisting a rush to scapegoat defeated generals, and another time refusing to collaborate with a bloody coup in an Athens humiliated by its rival Sparta. Still, Socrates was undeniably, to his fellow citizens, a troubling presence as a skeptic and dissenter and, what may be more, as a man detached from the interests and passions of his neighbors and even friends. It's as if one of us were scornful, let's say, of the deeply held religious convictions of all those around us or, more pointedly still, indifferent to their shared sense of outrage and vulnerability after some great national defeat.

Many years after Socrates' death, an orator named Aeschines mentioned that Socrates had been executed because he taught, among many others, a tyrant named Critias. Thus some have argued that the real reason for Socrates' execution was that he taught his students to mock the democratic constitution of Athens. When that constitution was overthrown, by Critias and others, Socrates neither protested nor rebelled, critics say.[2] Indeed, he lived more or less safely for months under the dictatorship of the Thirty, while many others died or fled.

Again, Socrates has an eloquent defense of both his action and inaction. Socrates tells this story: the Thirty tyrants ordered him and others to seize a man named Leon from the outlying village of Salamis and bring him into the city for what was bound to be an assassination. This happened all too often under the dictatorship. The Thirty killed hundreds of Athenians, often seizing the property of the murdered for themselves. But, Socrates tells us, "the regime, with all its might, did not scare me into doing injustice. . . . The four others went to Salamis to bring Leon back but I went straight home. . . . And for this I might well have been put to death," had not the dictatorship itself fallen.

Philosophy students have argued for centuries about whether Socrates did

---

2. Mostly notably, I. F. Stone in *The Trial of Socrates*.

the right thing. Leon was murdered after all; Socrates was innocent of that murder, of course. These are plainly judgments based on facts. Still, most of us feel there's little heroism in going home to safety while thugs and cowards murder someone who might have been saved had we only warned him.

The account that Plato gives of this one incident from Socrates' long life can serve as a kind of pivot on which to turn and ask a question about you and me and all of us. Study and inquiry have often been seen as reflective, contemplative, even passive, in relation to the world of action, politics, heroism. Plato's writing shows this clearly. In his greatest work, *The Republic*, Plato describes the constitution of the state as like the constitution of the soul. He divides the soul into three parts, using the metaphor of three kinds of lives, each representing an aspect of our souls: most people seek wealth, he says; some seek chiefly honor or glory; and some others, perhaps very few, seek knowledge, and with it virtue or goodness. Plato may well have taken this division from an older school of mystical mathematical thinkers who surrounded the great Pythagoras. Among these Pythagoreans it was also said that we had to choose among three sorts of lives. We could see the choice clearly in the people who crowded into the city for the annual athletic contests. "Some come to compete for fame and glory," they said. "Some come to make money by selling and buying things. But some come only to watch." Oddly, at least to us, it was in the spectators that the Pythagoreans found a proper image for themselves as students, as philosophers.

I know that passivity is not the right word for contemplation. Aristotle said that contemplation was the most active of all our mental states. Contemplatives in many, many faiths have agreed. It is not passivity they seek, but detachment.

Still, detachment in politics and civic life can be a form of passivity. Take voting as a simple example. Less than half of Americans vote these days. Among college students, only a quarter vote.

I doubt that it is the most philosophical, the most contemplative, who stay home on election day. I suspect the reasons are much more ordinary: laziness perhaps; indifference to the issues; postponement of adult responsibilities. But there is one motive that may link up to the intellectual life you have led as students: it is cynicism, a sense, a perfectly rational and sophisticated sense, that individual votes make little or no difference.

In a society as large and powerful as ours, one so full of contradictions, it's easy to lose hope in change, in the effectiveness of your own efforts against large social forces, forces that can more easily be steered with fibs and fears than with complex truths. The sheer size of our country, its enormous economic and military power, may contribute to a sense of futility: who am I, you may wonder, to protest or complain about the actions of the mightiest state in human history? How often can one person, or even a handful, turn around policies in an Athens, never mind in an America?

The insecurity and anxiety that we have all felt since September 11, 2001, only intensify the sense that futility haunts our best efforts to build good lives for ourselves and for others.

Recently we went to war twice to make the world safe—or safer—from terrorism. We debated and still debate the politics, economics, and morality of these relatively small but violent engagements. The debate continues: no doubt it will go on for years. There may well be more wars to come with equally uncertain outcomes and equally unresolved debates.

Can such debates make a difference? The temptation from cynicism is to say, as with voting, that none of this talk makes any difference at all. Wars are fought now by specialists, few of whom you will know or influence as your lives and careers unfold. Policy experts in Washington seem to make the key decisions; some of you may join them as the years go on; but necessarily most of you will have little contact with them or their world of think tanks and political appointments. The president of the United States, elected by an increasingly small fraction of those who might vote, has little or no time for the sorts of debates or protests that make campus life interesting.

So as you move on you will be tempted to say, "What's the use? All that talk was a kind of educational exercise; now I have better things to do...."

You will turn away not so much to go home to safety as to go on with work on a scale where you can achieve concrete and measurable results, for yourselves and for others.

The turn makes sense for most of us. But I worry that it represents a surrender of the hope that through democracy we can change history, even a little. One case pushes against my own temptation toward detachment or cynicism. On May 8, 2002, an American citizen named José Padilla returned to the United States from abroad, traveling from Pakistan to Switzerland and then on to Illinois. As he got off the plane, at O'Hare Airport outside Chicago, he was arrested by federal marshals. At first, he was held as a material witness for a grand jury in New York investigating terrorism. But on June 9, 2003, President Bush ordered that Padilla be held henceforth as "an enemy combatant" associated with Al Qaeda. He was transferred to a Navy prison in South Carolina, where he remains today.

Except for the presidential statement, Padilla has never been charged with a crime to which he might plead innocent or guilty. For two years lawyer or relative could see him.[3] Petitions of habeas corpus filed on his behalf have all been denied on appeal. Newspapers tell us about his childhood and family, his criminal records, and his conversion to Islam and adoption of an Arabic name. Statements from officials suggest that he was followed overseas by intelligence agents. These agents report that he trained with Al Qaeda to plant "dirty" nuclear bombs here at home.

José Padilla may well be guilty, as President Bush, Secretary of Defense Rumsfeld, and others suggest. The question that nags at me—and the question that should nag at us all—is the one your teachers have put to you again and again in the spirit of Socrates: How do we know that? How can we be sure of it? Have we listened carefully to those—like Padilla or his lawyers—who might disagree?

Under our Constitution, under our laws, we seek answers to such questions through what we call due process, that is, hearings and trials before

---

3. He did see a court-appointed lawyer, however, when first transferred to New York.

judges, evidence and arguments presented by lawyers. Socrates defended himself in an ancient version of due process. But our country is grievously threatened, as we all know, and the threat forces hard choices on us as a people. It is, I think, an important and valid question just where and when we may have to suspend or postpone these processes so as to secure our safety.

During the Civil War, President Lincoln suspended the writ of habeas corpus. In a case in Indiana, a troublesome man named Milligan challenged the president's power to use military courts to try Americans like himself.[4] His argument was the simple one that citizens of the United States were entitled to appear before civilian judges and juries, rather than military officers, even in wartime. The Supreme Court held that the government could not do this "where the courts are open and their process unobstructed." And thus Milligan was released.

Does this principle, should this principle, apply now to José Padilla? He is an American citizen, born in Brooklyn and reared in Chicago. The courts are "open and unobstructed." But, again, the nation faces threats we have never known before.

Padilla is said by experts to be a terrorist enlisted in an enemy force. One of the most important precedents in this area of constitutional law was decided by the Supreme Court in 1942. In the midst of the Second World War, the Court upheld the conviction and execution of seven German soldiers, all of them onetime residents of the United States fluent in English.[5] They had landed from submarines on beaches in Long Island and Florida, buried their uniforms, and headed toward towns and cities with orders to sabotage bridges and factories. Like Padilla, they did not get far. (Unlike him, they were not fanatics and quickly lost their nerve.) Chief Justice Stone said, in upholding their military execution, that unlike Milligan they had violated "the laws of war" and thus could be tried and convicted by military tribunals.

These precedents do not close off the questions raised by the Padilla case: Can citizens of the United States be arrested on the say-so of high officials?

---

4. Ex parte Milligan, 71 U.S. 2 (1866).
5. Ex parte Quirin, 317 U.S. 1 (1942.).

Can they be held indefinitely in military detention? Can they be convicted and punished by the military rather than civilian authorities when the civilian courts are "open and unobstructed"? When the nation is at peace, the answer to these questions is clearly no: we are all entitled to the elements of due process from American courts. When the nation is at war, as in these two cases, the answer may well be more difficult.

Our own situation partakes of both war and peace: we have enemies who have or seek to have the weapons of war; we will have such enemies for a long, long time. Yet the nation is in nothing like the disorder and desperation of the Civil War nor the urgency, the stringency, that obtained during the great wars, the world wars of the twentieth century. Padilla, whatever wrong he did or planned to do, was and is an American citizen. Like the German soldiers, he may well have enlisted with an enemy army, and what is worse, a covert terrorist army.

But the question for us—the question for you—is whether our security needs have become so urgent that we need to suspend due process, suspend the Bill of Rights, so as to make the nation safe from terror. If so, any one of us must be ready to be imprisoned without a hearing on the secret report of intelligence and defense authorities.

Socrates may have turned away from the execution of Leon of Salamis. He would not have turned away—he did not turn away—from questions such as these, about the fairness of our laws and the justice of our wars and executions.

I urge you, then, to take up these questions. Neither I nor anyone else can decide them for you. You must debate them; you must vote them; above all, you must take them up on your own. Take them up with a conviction, with a faith, that your thoughts, your arguments, your actions, will shape America in the years ahead. Your active, Socratic citizenship can contribute, in ways large and small, to justice in the United States and around the world.

When Socrates was executed in Athens in 399 B.C., his nation, small as it was, stood threatened by both conquest and subversion. America now, and in your lifetime, is not likely to be threatened by either. But Athens, like

America, was under a kind of siege. For one reason or another, and partly in self-defense, it had become an empire, if a very small one. We in America are not a true empire, though many say we are becoming one. Certainly, we have a kind of military and economic dominion that few of the world's empires could ever claim.

What I take from Socrates—what I hope you will take from the liberal arts—is not passivity or detachment but the conviction that even in the midst of great danger we should never fear questions and arguments.

Will our actions make any difference to America and to the world? The cynic in each of us will say no: it's a big and busy world, a stubborn world, and one not likely to listen to you or me as we debate or protest or vote.

There is an act of faith in all action. You came to college in that faith; so did I. May your faith remain strong—and stubborn.

Just War

No celebration can take place unless we are willing to put aside, for a while, matters that we cannot celebrate. This is a harsh rule but, as I see it, a binding one. A birthday, a birth, a marriage, a graduation: we find a place in our lives to celebrate these moments, knowing they will soon rush on into the great current of the rest of our lives. So we put out of mind, for a few hours, what makes us sad or angry or just perplexed. Among the many difficult matters that we put aside at graduation, surely the most public one is the war in Kosovo—or more exactly the two wars, NATO's air war on all of Yugoslavia and the all-but-completed Yugoslav war on the Albanian Kosovars. It still seems odd to me to say that our country is at war. Daily life in America bears few signs of wartime austerity or anxiety. On campuses there are neither protests nor rallies, and we go on with our lives taking notice of the war in an occasional conversation or, as here, a serious teach-in on the issues that have brought us to this awful impasse. The calm seems preternatural when I

CITIZENSHIP

reflect that we have been at war with another nation, with Yugoslavia, for the better part of a semester.

So I'm going to intrude, then, with just a few sentences about this war and its meaning in our lives—particularly in your lives as young citizens of this and many other countries.

It is just, and even urgent, as I see it, to resort to reasonable and proportionate means to save the Albanian or Muslim population of Kosovo from the violence of the Yugoslav military and paramilitary forces. That violence, with its reminder of what happened in Bosnia, has given us a new name in the long human catalogue of horror: we call it "ethnic cleansing." It happened in Rwanda not very many years ago, and we did, effectively, nothing to stop it. It is an age-old practice of our species on every continent, including our own. Many of us see in it a near relation to genocide. Kosovo is only the most recent and visible exercise of this age-old practice.

I am struck by how readily we can imagine the violence in a valley like this one, with farms and small towns and high hills. The army, from positions on nearby hillsides, first shells the farms and villages with artillery. They then enter the villages to tell the residents to leave their homes more or less immediately, taking next to nothing, sometimes leaving the sick or handicapped behind. The army often separates out the men of fighting age—from fifteen or so to fifty. These men, as far as we can learn, are soon killed or taken as hostages. Murders of all sorts take place with a randomness that terrorizes the new refugees: a baby here, an old person there, someone who moves too slowly or who is resented by a neighbor. Young women, as in Bosnia, are often taken away to be raped. Bribes are extracted at every turn for small mercies in the midst of this terror.

How much of it is still going on? Skeptics and journalists can and should ask this question. We may never know the answer. We know enough to say that it is the systematic policy of the Yugoslav military and police in Kosovo Province under the direction of leaders in Belgrade. It is calculated to drive the Kosovars away forever. In that calculation, as we all know, success is near at hand for Milosevic and his supporters. Against all of this—whether in

Kosovo, in Tibet, or in Rwanda—we can, I believe, find a just cause. Against it, we can, that is, fight a just war. But with equal seriousness and passion I will say to you here that I do not believe that we are now engaged in a just war.

I offer this view as my own, in a spirit of openness and not of dogmatism or coercion. I offer it to you as if to say: you, too, should have—must have—views on this. War is capital punishment on a great, international scale. We cannot, as citizens, say we are indifferent to it because it does not affect our daily lives.

As understood over centuries by philosophers, notably Thomas Aquinas, a just war is just only if it meets three important conditions: it requires, first, a just motive or principle. We have such a principle in Kosovo. But philosophers like Aquinas say that a just principle is never sufficient to warrant the moral judgment that particular actions are just. We must impose at least two other conditions: first, and most bluntly, a war to be just must also be winnable. No one should wage war, even for a just end, if the end cannot be realized because the war itself has little or no chance of success. In the case of Kosovo, our estimation of the probability of success in war depends to a large extent on our willingness to risk our own resources and the lives of our own soldiers—mostly young men and women of precisely college age.

But this brings us to the third and most telling of these three principles: a war to be just must be fought by means both effective and proportionate—effective in bringing about the just end of the war *and* proportionate, in cost or degree of violence, to the evil we seek to end. Simply put, this third test comes to this question: is the inevitable evil of war for a just cause—the evil of death and destruction visited on the other side (or both sides)—is that inevitable evil clearly less than the evil for which we go to war in the first place? Wars, all wars, do harm we never imagined when begun. They kill civilians. They kill soldiers. They kill those we hoped to protect.

The Kosovo war, as we are now conducting it, poses few risks to allied soldiers. As an American, I would like to cheer that fact. I have four sons from twenty four to fourteen, and I would not want to risk any of them in war. I would want to be sure, very sure, that a war was truly just and urgent before

I could vote to risk the lives of my own children and my own students, of you and your classmates and contemporaries across the land. But the three necessary conditions of Aquinas would seem to suggest that if we are sure that we have a just cause for war, then we fight it, bravely, in the most effective and proportionate way: that we fight it, that is, so as to win by those means best calculated to spare lives on all sides and to minimize the inevitable evils of a just war. Many on and off this campus who know much more than I about the Balkans do not believe that a just and successful war to save the Kosovars can be fought, realistically, by the United States or by NATO. Democracies have many virtues, but they do not make such sacrifices lightly. Our democracy in particular, for all its power and wealth, confronts a world full of evils, even at home. We cannot do everything well; we cannot prevent every evil; we have neither the patience nor the willingness to outlaw ethnic terror on every continent. And we have some trouble facing up to our own hatreds and the violence within our own society.

The war in Vietnam, as you know, began without much fanfare in the United States: a few hundred and then a few thousand soldiers, called advisors to those we supported in the south. Several years later, it had become a great and awful conflict, with many, many deaths among our soldiers, many more among theirs, and with awful, evil, deaths inflicted, sometimes by accident, sometimes not, on the civilian population north and south. I won't go into the reasons for that war. Enough has been said about whether or not it was a just war.

What I will say about the war in Vietnam is this: because of the draft, because our soldiers might be drawn from all quarters, the Vietnam War "came home," above all on campuses. The draft forced each of us to confront the war and to take a stand.

Now, thirty years later, we have taken the momentous step of giving up on what we used to call a civilian army. Our military is now professional, volunteer: no one joins unless he or she chooses to join. What this means to you is that you can, in fact, shrug off wars, leaving it to our leaders in Washington and to your contemporaries who have joined the military to sort out the great ambiguities and uncertainties of what we are doing. But Kosovo is the future. History is not over, nor is hatred or nationalistic passion. There will be more Kosovos. There are more now than we acknowledge.

Partly because of the war in Vietnam I read, at your age, all that I could find on the morality of war. Among the philosophers who wrote most powerfully on this was a young Frenchwoman who died in exile during the Second World War. Her name was Simone Weil. She believed, to her peril, that she had to confront in person the great evils on which, as a citizen and philosopher, she would pass judgment. So she went to Spain during the civil war there; she worked among the migrant agricultural workers in the south of France; with her doctorate from the Sorbonne in hand she took a job in the worst factory she could find. During the Nazi occupation she joined the Free French forces in England and tried, quite ineffectively, to help the resistance in France. Perhaps Simone Weil's finest writing was about war.

In agonizing over the violence of war, she suggested a moral test for killing. A sometime pacifist, she nonetheless believed that violence was needed at times to stop evil. Anyone who kills in war, she said, must ask if justice so requires the death of this person, this enemy, that you would choose that death even if it were you yourself or someone you loved who would be the one to die by your actions.

What she suggests is a test of our courage in going to war. And I would add that test of courage to the three conditions for a just war. We should never kill unless we believe that our cause justifies not only killing, but dying.

None of us here has the power to resolve this crisis in Kosovo. And all of our bombs have not thus far saved the lives and homes of the Kosovars. But all of us bear some responsibility as citizens for what has happened, what is now happening, and what will go on happening.

If the cause is not just, or it is impossible, or unwinnable, then we should stop what we are doing. If it is just, then we must, as a nation, be much braver than we have been and risk our own lives along with those of the Serbs and the Kosovars.

During your four years here, many of you, more times than I can count, told me that you regretted the apathy of your generation, its lack of great public passions, of great causes. I didn't agree with you about all this when you argued it. I found in the charge a little too much nostalgia and romance for what was, after all, the youth of your parents and teachers and people like me. But today I take up your argument. All of us need to weigh the questions put by Kosovo and this war. They are simple and they are urgent. And they will be with us, with you, for years and years to come.

Who is our neighbor? When do we come forward to stop violence and persecution against her or him? What price are we willing to pay to help the refugees and the victims of hatred or cataclysm? Finally, most solemnly, when does justice compel us to go to war and to risk our lives for others? If college prepares you for anything, it prepares you to take on questions like these. As you go away, as you go on in your lives, I celebrate in this very serious way your passion for learning and for wisdom. The world has need of you.

Patriotisms

My father and I had lots of arguments when I was in college, about lots of things: Was capitalism moral? Was wealth? Was the government in the hands of evil people? Usually we fought on the phone, but not always. Sometimes we hung up laughing; sometimes we hung up in grim disagreement. Once he told me that I shouldn't bring my girlfriend Adelia home because she was anti-American. I hung up on him that night and for two weeks we didn't talk at all. During all my undergraduate years, in the latter half of the '60s, we had plenty to fight about because of the war in Vietnam.

The best of these fights with my father—the most difficult and instructive—were the ones where he reached back into his own life to draw a lesson for me, often one that I resisted or refused. Then we could compare lives, or at least what we imagined our lives to be about.

One thing we could never agree on was what he called "service to one's country." "When your country asks you to serve," he said, "you don't say no." His voice was intense and vulnerable in saying this to me. He seemed to put aside arguments about effective methods of protest, or about the justice or injustice of the war itself. He wanted to assert something much more basic, perhaps to him the most basic principle of all: you serve your country when your country—through its laws, its policies—says it needs you. You don't ask questions; you don't say no.

This was my father's idea of patriotism. It was an idea he shared with nearly everyone who came of age during the Second World War. It was unquestioned and, for the most part, it was unquestioning.

In his case the idea had added force because he had not been able to serve during the war. In those days he had terrible asthma. It went away only in his late middle age. Throughout my childhood he had terrifying attacks, falling down wheezing, barely able to breathe for minutes at a time. In 1941, just after Pearl Harbor, he had enlisted in the Navy and made it to officers' training school. An attack of asthma there led to a medical review and an involuntary but honorable discharge. He tried the Army, but they found out about the asthma and rejected him too. He went through the war yearning to serve. Then his youngest brother, Ricky, was killed on the last day or two of the war in Germany: he was barely eighteen. Ricky's death seemed to close off forever any argument about patriotism and the duty to serve one's country. These were absolute imperatives for my father, made all the more absolute because his youngest brother seemed to him to have died in his stead.

Patriotism suggests many things, but none more clearly than love of country. The question we must all face as citizens of this and other countries is what to make of that love—or the lack of it—in ourselves and in others. Is it necessary? Does it impose duties of service? Can they be questioned or challenged? What sort of patriotism do we need now?

Patriotism is a sentiment much more than it is an argument. As a sentiment it can grow into a passion, sometimes a dangerous uncontrollable passion. Still, it is an important sentiment, and one that most nations nurture and encourage.

Most of us who are Americans have felt our patriotism achingly, overwhelmingly, during the time after the terrorist attacks of September 11, 2001.

The first lesson about patriotism is that it cannot be imposed or required. No sentiments can be compulsory, not even such basic sentiments as love of family or love of nation. Our history and the way we understand it will condition each of us to feel what we feel, in whatever complicated variants there are on the love and passion around us.

Compare what I felt during the Vietnam War with what my father felt during the Second World War. Both were expressions of patriotism. Mine took the form of enormous anguish about what my country was doing in Vietnam. I had heard the arguments for service, for war, and I had made some of them myself at the outset, in 1964, as a senior in high school and a freshman in college. Resisting a communist takeover, especially in the South, seemed a worthy and democratic end: the communists would not allow elections, or free speech, or freedom of worship; they would create a permanent tyranny. America represented democracy and freedom—and the willingness, as Kennedy had suggested in his inaugural, "to pay any price, to bear any burden. . . ."

But by the time I was a sophomore in college, this simple view seemed more and more untrue to what we were doing: our allies in South Vietnam were not pure democrats; many of them were corrupt, and some were cowardly. Our enemies in the North were not only communists but nationalists, patriots, asserting the right of the Vietnamese to rule themselves without French or American protectors.

Sorting all this out, as best I could, I felt that I wanted to serve my country (as well as the people of Vietnam), but in a just and effective way. My father's rule—that when your country asks, whatever it asks, you give it—that rule seemed to me not just wrong, but disastrously wrong.

By comparison, my father's generation, despite the great risks they took and the great sacrifices they made, saw few ambiguities in patriotism and the call of military service. For them there was good and there was evil: Hitler and his allies were, as Churchill called them, "monsters of evil" representing a "new dark age" for Europe and the world.

You bear a curious relation to the generation that fought Hitler. Some say that your challenges are similarly unambiguous, that you must resist evil, go to war against it. But most of us are uneasy about this analogy. The evil that we have identified is not a nation or a religion or even precisely a political movement. It is a technique: terrorism, the killing of civilians to make a political point or achieve a political end.

Against this evil, there is no one method of struggle and no sure policy. Our country will not ask you to serve in the manner of the Second World War or of Vietnam. The military is a separate and specialized profession now, one constituted by volunteers, recruits, who have joined on their own and without compulsion, without a draft. We honor those, including classmates, who serve in this way, but they cannot be many—and they cannot carry all of the burden of patriotic service.

How then can you and I serve? If we feel patriotism, then what are we to do with it, how are we to express it, and what are its duties?

First, I would say with my father that we owe an allegiance to our country and that patriotism is a nearly inescapable sentiment. Some of you are citizens of more than one country; others are citizens of countries other than the United States. So the question arises not so much of patriotism but patriotisms: might the world do better to rid itself of national feeling, of national loyalties and passions?

This is a powerful idea and one that may tempt many of you.

In 1900, as an old man, his great novels and stories long behind him, Tolstoy wrote a passionate denunciation of "the hypnotism of patriotism. . . ." It is, he said, "an unnatural, irrational, and harmful feeling, the cause of a great part of the ills from which mankind suffers. . . ." Patriotism should be "suppressed and eradicated by all rational means. . . ." He had in mind, I think, the way patriotism can lead on to fanaticism, to ideas of tribal purity and tribal triumph.

As an antidote to this poison, the classicist Martha Nussbaum urges the creed of the Stoics. "I am a citizen of the world," Diogenes Laertius said, in Greek *a cosmou polites*, a cosmopolitan.

This is generous and noble, but is it workable? My own view is that the rejection of national loyalty is utopian and futile. There may be a few who can live without national attachments, as there are a few who can live without families. But most of us feel these national attachments deeply. The challenge, then, is not the utopian one of suppressing or eradicating patriotism, but the practical one, the political one, of disciplining it and making sense of it. If patriotism is an inescapable sentiment, as I think it is, then we must make good use of it (just as we seek to make good use of the passions we feel for friends, lovers, family).

Second, I would say, this time with Socrates (and perhaps, ever so gently, against my father), that our patriotism can never be unquestioning. There are times, we all know, when the quibbler and the hero part company. In emergencies, we need heroes—whether to fight a Hitler or to stop a terrorist. But in preparing for emergencies, and in the everyday work of citizenship, we need quibblers and questioners. Indeed, they too should be among our heroes.

The war against terrorism illustrates this. We can all agree on measures of security at airports and in skyscrapers and perhaps even at borders. We have much more trouble agreeing on what measures we can take—military, economic, political—to assure our children and grandchildren that we will leave them a human world better and safer than the one we now confront. It was said often during the war in Vietnam that we needed to win hearts and minds to our side. I will not be so naive as to adopt that slogan for present use. What is clear is that hardened hearts, fanatical minds, can now terrorize cities, nations, and the world. And none of us can say for sure that we know how to bring together, say, the Hindu and the Muslim, the Hutu and the Tutsi, the Protestant and the Catholic, the Arab and the Jew, the American and the anti-American.

It is uncomfortable, even infuriating, to entertain challenges and criticisms in the midst of war and emergency. But it will be much worse not to heed doubts about our policies in a prolonged and uncertain struggle. What should our nation stand for in the world? How prompt should we be in military response? What is the right balance between constitutional rights and emergency measures? What is the best way to counter the intoxications of patriotic and religious fervor?

Finally, I hope that yours will always be a *generous* patriotism. And I mean this in two senses: generous, first, toward others in their patriotisms, their national feeling and pride as Afghan or Turk, Ghanaian or Venezuelan, Palestinian or Israeli, as Americans of the right or Americans of the left. An ungenerous patriotism is one that denies to others what you seek for yourself and for your own nation or people. It is, at bottom, a chauvinism: me and my country over you and yours. But in a world as crowded with nations as ours, our patriotism—all patriotism—must be generous toward and tolerant of others. It must be restrained and respectful of the deep differences among peoples. To some this will seem an oxymoron, a sharp contradiction or absurdity. All patriotism is chauvinistic, they will say, with Tolstoy. But I myself hold for a disciplined and informed love of country, one rooted, no doubt, in emotion, but one improved by reason and thought—a love of country that rejoices in the love that others feel in turn for their countries.

There remains an additional and more particular sense in which this nation, America, requires a generous patriotism. Let me cite from a recent learned text: in the first Spiderman movie, the just bitten Peter Parker has a touching exchange with his Uncle Ben, an exchange that suits us and America both. "Knowledge is power," Ben says to Peter (who is about to discover his own power). "But with great power comes great responsibility." Uncle Ben echoes John Kennedy: "Of those to whom much is given, much is required."

This is the most powerful nation on earth. To a large extent, its knowledge—your knowledge—is also its power. It is also the richest nation the world has ever known. It is a generous nation, one that gives in many, many ways. But generosity, like patriotism, has its flood tides and its droughts. By some important measures, we have become ungenerous, abroad and even at home. "The great empire," St. Augustine once said of Rome, "is a great piracy. . . ." Our empire, in my view, is not a piracy; but nor is it the City of

God on earth. Two empirical measures stand out for me. Our nonmilitary foreign aid to poor countries, measured per capita or by overall wealth, is among the lowest of all the democratic and developed nations we look to as our close allies. It is a small fraction of what Japan or Denmark, Holland or France or Germany gives to poorer nations. This should not be so. It is not worthy of us or of our patriotism. A second measure is no less worrisome. Our economy has become, increasingly, an engine of prosperity and a model for the world. But its rewards have become, increasingly, skewed toward those of us who are educated and successful. I do not say that any simple reforms will bridge the gaps between rich and poor, here or abroad. But a generous nation, a responsible nation, in a position of overwhelming power and success, must prove to itself and to the world that it seeks to help all share in the earth's and humanity's wealth. To us then, and to you, much is given and much will be required.

TIME AND LOSS

Birch Beer

When I was five or six, I was allowed to walk down our road one summer day, through caverns of maple shade, to a rural gas station. There, with the help of my big brother, I could buy gumballs and candy. In the corner there was a small white refrigerator with sodas, all in glass bottles of different shapes and colors. (This was before the reign of plastic and aluminum.) The man who pumped the gas would sell this stuff with a casual indifference that I found unfathomable. He dispensed what to me were the rarest of treasures. In the cooler, as he called it, there was a clear soda in a simple bottle with plain writing on the glass surface. Birch Beer, it said, in block letters in white paint.

I had no idea who made it or what it was made of, but my brother told me to try it. He knew I liked root beer. There were birches in our yard with streaked bark. I had no idea how someone could make a soda out of a tree. I remember distinctly that I handed the man my dime as if it had been his all along, as if I were just returning it to him. I followed him over to the refrigerator; he opened the small door, leaned in toward the light inside, and picked out a bottle from among several on a middle shelf. He pointed out a red opener marked Coca-Cola on the side wall of the counter. I pried the top off the bottle slowly and awkwardly.

I lifted up the bottle and took what the bigger boys called a swig. There was tingle in my nostrils from the fizz, and the drink gurgled into my mouth. I gulped at its taste. When I put the bottle down on the counter I was disturbed to see that the circle at the surface had fallen by as much as an inch. Suddenly, this new wonder was finite, limited. With the next swig, and the next and the next, this bottle would soon be empty. I was shocked that this wonder would rush by so fast.

Time is a mystery to us. We know it by the way things change: you go off to high school as a slight fourteen-year-old, and you graduate looking very much like a grown-up; your *parents,* whose most vivid memories are of when they were sixteen or eighteen, look around at a graduation gathering and are astounded at how gray at the temples, how portly and wrinkled, not they but their contemporaries have become; even your *teachers,* those pillars of fixity in a changing world, even your teachers may have changed just a little in the time you have known them—one had a baby, another ran a marathon, one bought a new car or maybe just a new tie with flamingoes on it and a palm tree.

We all have personal clocks or measures for time. That bottle of birch beer was my first and most telling clock. It measured time in a way that mattered to me—as I now recall—beyond all other measures. I would imagine an endless bottle of birch beer, an unmeasured, unclocked pleasure, tasting of bark and trees and yet clear to the point of vanishing.

"The good and the beautiful have no enemy but time," said William Butler Yeats. All beauty is frail, Yeats wants to teach us, and all goodness too. We all know how quickly the blooms of the azaleas and daffodils give way in a month's time as spring gives way to summer. You know how quickly, by another measure, a child becomes an adult. At other times, in study hall or when a paper's overdue, time seems to lumber slowly toward some obscure end. Like the birch beer in the bottle, time is drunk—swigged—and gone.

Your time as students ends soon enough. In an old-fashioned way, with robes and speeches and song, your teachers will say: be on your way; you are done here; you have worlds to conquer; and you are ready.

For many of them, your leaving will come too soon. I know it will seem like ages to you, whether you started here a year ago or two or three or four years back. You were a different person then: your blue jeans were smaller, your hair shorter or longer, you didn't know Latin or calculus, and you'd never met the person you now think of as your closest friend in all the world. By a teacher's measure, all that was yesterday. The changes didn't cancel out the essential personality they said hello to long ago and will say good-bye to today. Though they may not always let on, they grow attached to you in a school like this one.

They have drunk with you from the same bottle of time. What you will remember of all this, tomorrow or the next day or ten thousand tomorrows from now, is not so much the slow lapping of time as you knew it here, as you read or wrote, slept or talked, exercised and argued; what you will remember is the marker, the birch beer bottle that you opened and closed together and that you called simply "school." "I went to school at a place called . . . ," you will say years from now to a new friend or a grandchild. There will be phrases about what you liked or disliked, about a favorite teacher or course, a game or performance or protest. These will sum it up, conclude it, put it away. Time—with all its oddities of change and continuity—time will be measured, and thus put behind you.

Time is what you have had together, you and your teachers and the rest of the school, and try as you will you can never capture time with these measuring devices, these second hands and minute hands and hour hands of memory and convention. "You were born the year after the war ended," my father used to say to me, "after Uncle Rickie died; the week the old Brooklyn Dodgers celebrated Durocher's fortieth birthday by winning their double header with the Pirates by a score of 4–3 in both games." "We graduated the year of the great mayhem in Bosnia," you will say. "The cities were in terrible trouble. We painted the bronze lion this color or that. *Cheers* ended the week before graduation."

The stretch of time before you now is special. You feel that, I'm sure. There's a special freedom in it. Choosing a college is a part of finding your way toward adulthood, toward choices of your own for work and friends and convictions. The time ahead will have special measures, too: freshman year, your major, falling in love in a way you never felt possible—and then another graduation. You cannot stop yourself from thinking about the markers along the way. They are what you aim at and work for. But once you reach one of these goals your mind will race ahead to the next of them. That's the nature of consciousness: it works like a hand grasping what's up ahead, pulling us towards it.

But it is the mystery of time—not its measure—that I want to remind you of as we mark off a portion of it. We set down measures to keep things in order: memory, work, children. These measures have no more intrinsic meaning than the empty bottle that once held my birch beer.

Consciousness is the only real measure, and it has not one clock, but an infinite variety of clocks, according to the things you will know, and feel, and bring into your lives.

But there is an end to consciousness. "This consciousness that is aware of neighbors and the sun," wrote Emily Dickinson, "will be the one that is aware of death." Out of the fact of death, and our knowledge of it, there is a great sadness to much of what we do—but also a great joy. I would not have cherished the birch beer quite so much had it not been such a small, rare, and finite dose of a kind of paradise.

The truth is that your consciousness of joy and sadness, your connection to it, in yourself and in others, is the great measure of time. And whether you have lots of time or little, a life that stretches out like Methuselah's or pulls in like that of the dying child in Sarajevo or Somalia, time is the same. It is yours to make of it what you will.

As you go on from here, and from *this* time in your lives, keep this little bit of joy and completion as a symbol of what you can make of *all* of your time. Fill it with friends, passions, love, and learning. Give yourself causes, and take them as far as you dare. Battle for what you believe in. Hold on to beauty. Rejoice in others and their battles and causes. And perhaps above all, drink time down with abandon and delight.

Time's Fog

When I was in seventh or eighth grade, I used to sit way in the back of the class, with other reprobates, and tune out the day's lessons. We had desks with wooden tops of yellow poplar. They folded up in front of you, making a kind of amber bunker or shield against the world and the nun at the front of the room. I took to hiding library books in the desk and reading them with the wooden top propped up on my wrists. I read a lot of science fiction then; I haven't read much since. I can't tell you the authors' names or the books' titles. I can remember what I saw in my mind—gray, rubbery planets with creatures of enormous suppleness and intelligence, shaped like playful cactuses. I can also remember themes, themes that in retrospect seem to me like those of the Odyssey: there were long wars, ambiguous victories, and, always, the grueling voyage home, a voyage full of terrors, and full, too, of a dread that home was not there anymore, that home was either gone forever or changed beyond recognition.

TIME AND LOSS

There is one story that is vivid to me still. This story told of a voyage in a time machine, a long voyage from the present to a distant past. The hero went back in time to set something right—to prevent a war or a plague. His adventure, perilous as it was, seemed to end well. Yet as he climbed back into his time machine he left something behind, quite by accident. It was a burnt-out match, I think. The forgotten match did no harm. It started no fire or cataclysm. But while it worked no obvious change in the world my hero had visited, it remained there, nonetheless, as a small alteration in time. And through some chain of unknown events, over the millennia, that cold, forgotten match altered the future.

"There isn't anything anywhere that doesn't make some difference somewhere," wrote William James. The discarded match my time traveler left behind was to utterly change the future to which he hoped to return. At the end of his voyage back, this modern Odysseus found that he was not returning home at all. His home in the future was gone, altogether gone. As he approached the point on his time chart where it should have been, he found that it was not there—and never had been. At the end of the story he himself had forgotten that it ever existed.

This story speaks to me still, mythically, of the great uncertainty of our intervention in time and history.

This year, we as a nation engaged in a short, hard war.* It involved a few of my former students and a half-million others, the greatest American troop deployment since Vietnam. We won, unambiguously, at a great cost in lives, although not American lives. That victory brought us, the victors, little that we had predicted and much we had not. We drove an occupying army from Kuwait; that much is certain. But neither the emir nor his people seemed to know where the government of Kuwait, or Kuwait as a nation, should go. We destroyed several armies of Iraq and the armaments we feared in that country. And for some of Iraq's people, the Shiites in the

---

* 1991: The first American invasion of Iraq.

south and Kurds in the north, our victory brought with it an opportunity for rebellion. But the rebellion was crushed, and a great army of refugees has now assembled in its wake.

We do not know what will come of our war in the Gulf. We will not know for a long time. Our efforts there reveal the vast uncertainties of war. Perhaps they give us a hint of the uncertainties of all human struggle.

You will find in your own lives that similar uncertainties attend all that you undertake. If disaster comes, it's usually without much warning. But it's also true that you will rarely be able to predict the small miracles and revelations by which you and others find a way toward fulfillment. Everything we set out to do is attended by the possibility of surprise, for good or ill, and sometimes for both.

You cannot cease from action because of life's uncertainty. Inaction is itself an unpredictable and uncertain ingredient of the future, like my hero's discarded match. In the Bhagavad Gita, the great Sanskrit scripture, there is a mysterious injunction: seek not the fruits—the results—of your own actions. Yet you must act, the scripture says.

My charge, then, is this: act, in your lives, act boldly, courageously, joyfully, but act without dogmatism, without the illusion that the future you reach toward is the one you will grasp, the one you had in mind. It is not, and it cannot be. What you set out to find, you will not find. Set out all the same, with your ideals strong and sturdy. But set out humbly, as time travelers, knowing that you cannot know what fruits your actions will bring.

Generations

The year I got out of college, my girlfriend, who was a little younger, dropped out to join what was called the Venceremos Brigade. This ragtag brigade was off to Cuba to cut sugar cane in defiance of the blockade. The harvest, *la zafra,* was going to be the biggest in history. It was going to bring Cuba new wealth and new possibilities. There was defiant talk that it would end the blockade somehow. I liked the idea that Adelia would go, but I worried that something bad might happen. It was not the illegality of the trip to Cuba that worried me. That made it interesting. The year was 1969, and everything interesting and important seemed to be against the law. I worried that she would love Cuba and want to stay. I worried, not unreasonably, that the Cuban boat would sink en route. Maybe I worried she'd meet someone else. But I had no grounds to object: just before I met her I had spent a dropout year of my own in a squatter settlement outside Lima, Peru.

She left from St. John's, Newfoundland, in a small, rusty freighter that shipped cattle among communist countries. The boat could easily have sunk; with every weather report I worried that it would. But the *brigadistas* made it ashore in Havana and were sent out to the country to cut cane. Adelia did love Cuba. The women insisted on cutting when the Cuban authorities said it was men's work. Fidel Castro came out to the fields to speak. Adelia spoke good Spanish and got to use it with Cuban students and farmworkers. She was impressed by the schools and the clinics in all the villages and towns. She liked the fresh ice cream that Castro bragged about. She didn't always like the way some of the Americans behaved; she didn't like the way some of the Cubans explained away the dictatorship and the punishment of dissent. She had her doubts, but mostly, at twenty, she was caught up in the fervor of socialist conviction that she found among Cuba's young communists.

Soon enough she was back home in Boston, where I was in law school, and we talked endlessly about what she had felt and seen. One of the funniest things about this time in our lives was the comments made about the *brigadistas* on the floor of the United States Congress while the boat was returning to St. John's. The newspapers reported outrage that this group of student dropouts had managed to evade the blockade and contribute their labor to what turned out to be the disappointing (and deflating) Cuban harvest of sugarcane. The outrage bordered at times on a charge of treason. But the officials who spoke seemed to recognize immediately that the *brigadistas* were going to come and go unpunished. "How dare they do this under our noses?" senators and representatives asked. Senator Eastland of Mississippi stood up and gave the best of these speeches to his colleagues. "These students," he said, "are human guided missiles aimed at the heart of America."

Adelia and I loved that comment and still recite it to one another at odd times of family misadventure. Somebody in authority, however preposterous, took them seriously and saw the threat of subversion in Adelia's otherwise uneventful return to me and to college.

I tell you this in order to touch on some of the things that authorities are saying about you: human guided missiles yourselves as you leave campus, aimed at something or other, I'm sure, out to do mischief of one kind or another; but few of us (and maybe fewer of you) know exactly what kind of mischief you are up to and how and when you will accomplish it.

Older people have talked about younger people for as long as we know. Often, older people seem to have assumed that things were better—even bigger—before. We call you a generation and affix various general attributes to you as a group: you are smarter, lazier, more sophisticated, less intense—or maybe intense about different things. Amid all these casual opinions, no one is ever quite sure how long a generation lasts or how widely our generalizations about generations apply. But we have become enormously self-conscious about the succession of generations: the greatest generation, the generation of the baby boomers, Generation X and Generation Y or Z.

What sense is there in this talk of generations, and what does it mean to you?

I was born in 1946, the first year after the end of the Second World War. Somewhere along the path of my childhood, a grown-up realized how many of us there were and first spoke of the baby boom. Kindergartens were crowded; suburbs sprouted everywhere; when the time came to apply to college, there were enough of us so that colleges and universities could pick and choose—and so began the "selectivity" in admissions that has dogged you and your generation through high school and college. More recently, people began to drop the "baby" in the epithet of my generation and refer to us all as "boomers": an appropriate word for lots of reasons, but perhaps most of all for its suggestion of boosterism and bluster, of a certain tinny tone of "here I come, so make plenty of room for me" that we in my generation have managed to sound in our every transition.

You can oppose your generation; you can lead it; you can revel in its company or you can despise it. But for better or worse these are your colleagues in time across the world. And wherever you live, and whatever you do, these are your neighbors—literally, those nearby.

Most of you were born to parents born at least two or three decades before. Together you are a cohort in time, a generation. People have described you in various ways:

TIME AND LOSS

There is the complaint—generations old, I suspect—that you are apathetic, that is, that you lack passion or commitment. There is the complaint that you are a generation of résumé builders, intent on your own fulfillment at work and in leisure but indifferent to the larger social good. The neoconservative David Brooks says that most of you put no emphasis on character and thus lack not just passion but ethics. Liberals and those on the left see you in much the same light, only lacking concern for inequality and injustice in the world at large.

I hear you say of yourselves that you find too little outrage among your classmates, or even in yourselves.

I'm uneasy with this sort of generalizing, even as I accept not just its inevitability but its possible bits of truth. There is implicit in it a kind of censure or blame: you are responsible for the sins not just of your fathers and mothers but of your companions within this generation.

If anyone can take responsibility for you and your generation it must be those who reared you and shaped you as children: your parents, your teachers, the singers you listened to, the writers you read, perhaps the politicians who led the country as you grew into adulthood. Maybe after all it is Mr. Rogers who's at fault; maybe his gentle way lulled you somehow into complacency. But I doubt it.

There's a wonderful statement of Lincoln's in the midst of his presidency: "I claim not to have controlled events; I confess plainly that events have controlled me." Events have controlled all of us: in our place of birth, the fortunes of those who reared us, the bodies we are, our temperaments—perhaps most of all in the advantages and disadvantages visited on us by the circumstances of our parents.

Talking to historians, I am convinced that we have in the idea of generations a notion owed to a certain kind of modern history or modern awareness—of time, of dates, of events. Europeans in the nineteenth century began to think of themselves not as ancients and moderns but as creatures of specific events and narrower periods: thus the generation of the Revolution in France, the generation of Napoleon, the generation of the uprisings of 1848 across the continent. Perhaps the most notable generation of the twentieth century was that of the First World War, which in its very naming suggested a notion of a global conflict and thus a widely shared experience. For many, perhaps for most, it was an awful experience, captured well in Ezra Pound's bitter elegy for Hugh Selwyn Mauberly. Pound wrote of the war's soldiers that they "walked eye-deep in hell, believing in old men's lies, then unbelieving came home. . . ."

Well before the modern period we read of generations, of course: there is the simple natural succession in a family line, as in the Bible's catalogue of who begat whom. There is a distinction among the sorts of people who have lived at different periods—"giants on the earth" or Methuselahs living to be 969.

By contrast, the notion of generations that we have grown used to seems absurdly casual. New generations are announced every few years, chiefly in America, often on the basis of fads or tastes, and rarely because of any large circumstance or event that frames lives. Generations thus identified may have no shared experience of anything but time—not war, not peace, not a hope or even, as with Pound, a despair. Still, there remain features of your experience that may put you, all of you, in a generation different from others before you. Let me evoke three of these:

First, you have grown up in an age of specialization. So has everyone before us, you may say. Specialization is relative and will go on forever. But the specialization that you have known has reached down into your lives early on and taken a hold on you beyond what any human beings have known before. Take sports, for a modest but telling example. Not only did the pick-up game disappear from childhood a long while ago, but so too did much of the free play that went with it. From an early age, your games have been coached and watched over by adults. Your play has been supervised and purposeful. In most cases, you were pushed, or pushed yourselves, to specialize in one game or another, to play it in all seasons, to compete in leagues and tournaments. One consequence is that you are often better than those of us who learned these games a generation ago. Another consequence is that you had less time to play—and more to train.

The example speaks, I suspect, to large portions of your lives: to your musical training, your intellectual lives, the careers opening up before you, perhaps in some sense even to your ties with those you love.

Second, you are the first generation in history to live in constant and instant connection to much of the globe. We who are your parents grew up with a widening web of travel connections to the world at large. That in itself changed the world, taking away remoteness and imposing a dominant world culture of marketing and trade on nearly every human settlement. But the web of computers and phones and faxes, with or without wires, has wrought an even more dramatic shift. At its best, it pushes us all toward world citizenship, toward an awareness of how different we all are and yet how alike. But at its worst, it makes us world-weary imperialists who can exploit anyone anywhere at any time. Around the world, those your age—or rather, the privileged among you—have more information and thus, in a narrow sense, more knowledge than any other human beings have ever had. This is a privilege, but it is also a huge, sometimes almost impossible, burden.

Third, and perhaps most decisive of all, you have grown up in an intellectual climate that is profoundly anti-utopian. Communism is dead; socialism is a modest corrective to capitalism; anarchism is an excuse for rioting or, worse, terrorism. The communes are gone; the kibbutzim are going. Many a revolution has come and gone, leaving a wrecked economy or a dictatorship in its place. Liberation struggles, like that of the Kosovars or the Afghans, can turn almost overnight into ethnic or religious tyrannies.

What is true, I think, is that you have grown up in a time that comes *after* many dreams, many utopias gone bad. If you are disillusioned, it is probably because some prominent illusions have fallen away. My generation can give names to our disillusion: Vietnam, Watergate, and then, with history going, as Marx predicted, from tragedy to farce, the various scandals and soap operas of American and world politics in the last few decades.

I have a sense that most of you knew this somehow in advance: you were wary of the illusions that lead to disillusionment and cynicism. You are cautious about utopian dreams, even in your own lives, because so many of them have led others to tragedy or comedy or both at once.

The challenge for you will be to make your way amid these conditions, shaped by them, but not bound by them. To work with others, you will have to specialize intensely. But in doing so, I hope you will find your way to a larger vision of what you are about, a vision in which your specialization makes sense and does good. Most of you will live lives of instant connection to a wild array of places and people. The challenge for you will be to forge a sense of responsibility across these great distances—and, what is harder, across the great differences of wealth, privilege, and power that will separate you from so many of your contemporaries. Finally, in an age that is too knowing for utopias, it will be up to you to hold out ideals against the cynicism that says that all ideals are fraudulent. The truth is that ideals can sometimes go wrong. But without ideals you will never find your way. The very conditions that will sometimes discourage you—the need for intense specialization, the global scale of competition and cooperation, the barrage of knowledge and information—these are the conditions that will test and strengthen your ideals and make them more powerful and more enduring.

It is always astonishing to be alive. For you to live now, when you can go anywhere and do almost anything, is an added source of astonishment. Yeats has a poem in which the gods envy those on earth their passions. We who are older may or may not envy you your youth, but we envy you the world you will come to know and to change.

Time and Loss

When graduation comes, with all its joys, it brings along also the sadness of an ending. It has a bittersweet taste of loss to it. I can sense it in the comments of parents and teachers: "It all went so fast." "I remember dropping you off," or "I remember you as a freshman the first day of class." At the end of the day, in the car, heading out on the road, some of you will recall your first glimpse of the Chapel or that room upstairs in the dorm with someone else's luggage and the unmade beds greeting you, a little bleakly, as you opened the door. What has gone so fast for you are the four years of college. For your parents there is a sense of loss as time's rush sweeps away your childhood. And for those of us who have taught you, we belong to a vocation in which each year we grow older and grayer but our students—as one class steps in for another—remain forever young.

In a poem that begins "A loss of something ever felt I," Emily Dickinson described herself as "[e]lder today, a session wiser, and fainter too as wiseness is." I want to say something about loss, and time, and how we wrest meaning from both of them.

My first protest, the first one I first remember, was of a loss I barely understood. I was alone in this protest. And I was protesting God. It happened this way:

I was small then. Not more than three or three and a half. My mother had a child who never made it home from the hospital. It was my first disappointment with life, with life itself, which promised in this instance a new sibling and then reneged.

I knew of the birth from the general hubbub in the house: my father wasn't there one night, as I recall, or my mother; they were at a hospital somewhere far away. Perhaps an aunt came by the house with the news. There was a babysitter who stayed with us, I'm sure, but I can't remember her name or face.

What I do remember is the quiet of the day on which we learned that the baby had died at the hospital. I was home alone with the babysitter; my older brothers were at school. I must have gotten up after they caught the school bus. I remember nothing of breakfast or the kitchen's stir of sandwich making and packing up for school. It was a bright day, warm, in the spring.

The babysitter told me that the new baby had died. I took this in without comment. She was a stranger; she might be lying, or at least mistaken somehow. I told her I would walk over to see our most neighborly neighbor, Mrs. McCann. The sitter must have called Mrs. McCann on the phone to tell her I was coming. There's a slight incline up to Mrs. McCann's old house. In those days there was almost no traffic. An old stone wall with brambles sidles along the grass strip by the country road. Mrs. McCann, an outspoken woman with a bluff, blunt way, stood in the road waiting for me. I treated it as a coincidence that she was there. "We have a new baby," I told her, "but the babysitter says it's not coming home. The babysitter's fibbing. It *is* coming home."

Whatever Mrs. McCann told me, it didn't make me cry. I'm sure she said a lot. I remember that I turned back with tears in my eyes but angry and not sobbing. I made my way to the front door. The babysitter was there. "I

TIME AND LOSS

believe you," I said. Then I hurried from room to room shutting the windows with a slam at each one. She tried to stop me. I'm shutting these to keep God out, I told her. He's mean; he took away the baby.

As I think back on it now, my window slamming was a kind of adjudication. I meant to set up a new boundary between God and me: I blamed Him for my loss and sent Him, as it were, to his room, outside the house. Even then, I must have suspected how brief an exile, how futile a punishment, this was. I never meant to spend the rest of my days (or even the rest of that one sunny day) inside the closed-up house, with meanness and perhaps time itself expelled outdoors. I know now that I was protesting not only God and loss, but growing up, too, with its frightening knowledge of mortality and vulnerability. In the few minutes from my denial and rejection of the babysitter's news to the moment when I accepted what Mrs. McCann said, I was growing up: by which I mean that I was learning that time means loss as well as gain—that I could not have the one without the other—and that blame is often of no help.

Death brushes up against us sometimes gently, sometimes roughly. At first, as a child, it may be a pet who dies or someone you never met. Sooner or later it is someone we love. I remember one spring when a wonderful student named Nishtha Adhvaryu took ill and died over the course of a few days. That same month we mourned the death of one of America's greatest twentieth-century poets, James Merrill, whose lifelong lyric theme was the paradox that nothing lasts and nothing ends.

Death takes someone away from us, but in doing so it reminds us of ourselves, our temporary, fragile selves. Again and again students remarked that spring on the death of their friend Nishtha as "drawing me up short" or "making me think differently about where I'm headed." They remembered her wit, her energy, her beauty; they remembered her alive and full of the emphatic, surprising detail of being alive; they remembered her in a midday class or at a muddy rugby practice; and then they knew that she was gone out of their lives with suddenness and without explanation. Or, rather, with only a medical explanation, which is more about a disease than about the person whom it visited so harshly.

TIME AND LOSS

The real death is never dramatic, James Merrill wrote when he was an undergraduate poet: "One night the heart embraces glass and dies, just so."

For most of us loss—great loss—turns our thoughts to whom and what we love, and to the shortness of our own time for loving and living.

When you set out, you are on a path, from home or college, that will not likely lead back the same way again, not often anyway. You think lots of thoughts then, at that moment, in that season of your life. One thought that few will evade is the suddenness with which a portion of your life concludes. And that leads on, for most of us, to the thought that all of life goes by quickly. It is a truism: everyone feels it from sixteen or seventeen on through old age.

Let me challenge its truth. Contrast your most vivid sense of the shortness of time with the many moments in which you have felt that something was taking much too long: a conversation you would rather not be in; a plane or train delayed by mechanical problems; a paper that you dreaded doing. No child who has ever faced an hour's drive would say that time is always short. Sometimes we itch with boredom at time's thick, slow spill toward a splash or finish of some sort. You know the feeling: I want out; I want to be done with this, to be elsewhere, with someone else, as someone else; I want to be different from what I am here and now. I am bored.

Boredom is a kind of hatred of the time and experience that are ours. Sometimes it comes of coveting another time and place not our own. Sometimes it comes of being trapped somehow where we should not be. Often it comes from our own laziness or inattention. Often we would not be bored if only we would listen up or pay more attention.

Wittgenstein once said of boredom that it's always our own fault. Time's rush is our fault, too.

We did not invent time; we discovered it—indeed, it must have been among the first discoveries. And we measured it, first through the changes in the natural world and later in the machines we made to measure natural things. We measured it so as to work with it, I am sure: for the harvest; the voyage; the pregnancy. But we may also have measured it so as somehow to hold on to it—to what we feel we have within its relentless passage of moment succeeding to moment. The end of college is a kind of marker, a noon or three o'clock, in your own measurement of time.

None of us can entirely dispense with the great clocks by which we measure our progress. We each have a story to live out, much as we cannot predict its end. We imagine our lives as if they had a script, an incomplete script, and we crave the cues to our upcoming lines and actions. Some psychologists have a notion that most of us repeat over and again, without much thought, a script from childhood that we find satisfying or justifying. My window-slamming was a script of sorts: it made sense of the harshness of my loss; it allowed me to punish (or to think that I had punished) the one I imagined behind it; and by exhausting me it allowed me to accept the final, irrevocable quality of loss.

Gestures of protest have an element of lyricism. We can understand them, like sacraments and poems, as efforts to shore up meaning against time and time's losses.

I have three simple reflections to offer from my childhood protest:

My first reflection is the simplest; it is about blame. I slammed the windows shut that morning because I was angry and blamed the one I took to be the perpetrator of my loss. It did me some good, as I have said. Later on, though, I or someone else had to open those windows up again. So I say to you: slam the doors and windows of your lives when you must. Protest because you have made a judgment and must voice it. But take more care in your blaming than I did. Make sure the target of your blame deserves it. And always, after a time, be sure to open up the windows and go back outside.

The second reflection is about time: Many of you are now planning the years ahead with a meticulous sense of how to accomplish your purposes: to become a scientist or teacher, a writer or entrepreneur; when to join your life with someone else's (or vowing now never to do so) or when (if ever) to have a child or a house or even an address for the Alumni Office. Many of you have plotted time's course, mapped it out like an explorer, so that you will reach a particular destination on a particular date and with the right supplies at hand. I will not fault you for your care. But I warn you against too much care for the map, and too little for the journey, with its infinite moments of passage.

I have often heard students say: I don't want to do this—medical school or a Ph.D. or pottery or film or what have you—because it takes too long. Two years is too long. Three is, or four or five. Too long for what? I wonder. What else is it that you would do? Those four or five years will go by one way or another, however you count them or eke them out.

"We must be light," Merrill wrote, "light-footed, light of soul, quick to let go. . . ." If you can let go of one moment so as to catch the next, time will bring you joys. Better, time's very passing will be itself a joy, as rivers are or fountains or the waves on the shore. So set your plans and purposes in time the way wanderers do; "I'm headed this way; I have a notion to do this and that; but I'm in no hurry; no one's waiting for me; I'll find my way—and my friends—as I go."

The last reflection is about loss: time will bring you losses; count on that. It will break your heart again and again, but the heart mends in time. And memory holds on, even—or especially—to what we lose. If loss teaches you anything, let it teach you to look to others, always, with a sense of how brief a time you share with them, and how vulnerable their lives and purposes are. Attend to them, then, with curiosity, with sympathy and, if at all possible, with affection. Where you must judge them, judge mercifully. "Who needs friends," Merrill asked rhetorically, "to remind him that nothing either lasts or ends?"

Treasure what you have, those you love, here and now. And treasure yourself, too, here and now, setting out from college, with ideas, with yearnings, with a script even, but with no fixed course, open to the world as the world is open to you.